Advance Praise for
It's Time for Strategic Scheduling

Scheduling is a crucial but oft-overlooked tool of school improvement. It gets approached as a mechanical chore rather than an opportunity for rethinking how schools can best serve students. In this pithy volume, Nate Levenson and David James bring a timely, practical, and long-overdue focus to helping school and system leaders do better.

—Frederick M. Hess
Senior Fellow and Director, Education Policy Studies, American Enterprise Institute

This is the book I wish I'd had as a principal, and I plan to put it in the hands of the school leaders I'm coaching as they wrestle with scheduling dilemmas. It's practical yet visionary, pushing our thinking on how to get the most from limited resources—both time and staff. It shares new research and approaches that will help readers rethink old questions, such as *does elementary reading always have to happen first thing in the morning? How can IEP meetings be orchestrated without pulling teachers away from their students? Is block scheduling better for student outcomes?* Scheduling is a powerful tool for improving school culture, teaching, and learning. This book will help improve any schedule.

— Kim Marshall
Author of The Marshall Memo

Levenson and James present a clear and focused pathway to ensure that your school schedule achieves your top priorities and supports student learning. Importantly, the authors provide a strong research base for scheduling and draw from decades of practical hands-on experience supporting schools to provide thoughtful and actionable recommendations. Anyone involved with school scheduling and staffing would benefit from this book and the practices it describes.

—Gabriel McCormick
*Senior Director of Teaching & Learning for Secondary Education,
Public Schools of Brookline (Mass.)*

IT'S TIME FOR
Strategic Scheduling

IT'S TIME FOR
Strategic
Scheduling

HOW TO DESIGN
SMARTER K–12 SCHEDULES
THAT ARE GREAT FOR STUDENTS,
STAFF, AND THE BUDGET

Nathan Levenson
David James

Arlington, Virginia USA

2800 Shirlington Road, Suite 1001 • Arlington, VA 22206 USA
Phone: 800-933-2723 or 703-578-9600 • Fax: 703-575-5400
Website: www.ascd.org • Email: member@ascd.org
Author guidelines: www.ascd.org/write

Richard Culatta, *Chief Executive Officer*; Anthony Rebora, *Chief Content Officer*; Genny Ostertag, *Managing Director, Book Acquisitions & Editing*; Susan Hills, *Senior Acquisitions Editor*; Mary Beth Nielsen, *Director, Book Editing*; Katie Martin, *Editor*; Thomas Lytle, *Creative Director*; Donald Ely, *Art Director*; Georgia Park, *Graphic Designer*; Circle Graphics, *Typesetter*; Kelly Marshall, *Production Manager*; Shajuan Martin, *E-Publishing Specialist*; Christopher Logan, *Senior Production Specialist*

All web links in this book are correct as of the publication date below but may have become inactive or otherwise modified since that time. If you notice a deactivated or changed link, please email books@ascd.org with the words "Link Update" in the subject line. In your message, please specify the web link, the book title, and the page number on which the link appears.

PAPERBACK ISBN: 978-1-4166-3206-1   ASCD product #123019   n7/23
PDF EBOOK ISBN: 978-1-4166-3207-8; see Books in Print for other formats.
Quantity discounts are available: email programteam@ascd.org or call 800-933-2723, ext. 5773, or 703-575-5773.
For desk copies, go to www.ascd.org/deskcopy.

Library of Congress Cataloging-in-Publication Data

Names: Levenson, Nathan, author. | James, David (Scheduling leader) author.
Title: It's time for strategic scheduling : how to design smarter K-12 schedules that are great for students, staff, and the budget / Nathan Levenson, David James.
Description: Arlington, Virginia USA : ASCD, [2023] | Includes bibliographical references and index.
Identifiers: LCCN 2023006338 (print) | LCCN 2023006339 (ebook) | ISBN 9781416632061 (paperback) | ISBN 9781416632078 (pdf)
Subjects: LCSH: Schedules, School. | Schedules, School—Economic aspects. | School management and organization. | School budgets.
Classification: LCC LB1038 .L52 2023 (print) | LCC LB1038 (ebook) | DDC 371.2/4—dc23/eng/20230308
LC record available at https://lccn.loc.gov/2023006338
LC ebook record available at https://lccn.loc.gov/2023006339

32 31 30 29 28 27 26 25 24 23   1 2 3 4 5 6 7 8 9 10 11 12

IT'S TIME FOR
Strategic Scheduling

Acknowledgments

Thanks to the many educators who have spent countless hours building schedules year after year. This book reflects many of their best practices, strategies, and insightful questions.

At ASCD, we wish to thank Katie Martin, our editor, for her expert guidance and suggestions and Susan Hills, who helped start the process to bring this book to life.

Finally, we thank our respective partners, Leslie Levenson and Sarah James, who both offered unending encouragement, patience, and support.

1

What Is Strategic Scheduling?

*How smarter schedules can supercharge
learning and engagement*

"I love our schedule!" the principal shouted with joy.

That's not something we hear very often. As consultants who work with elementary, middle, and high schools throughout the United States, we can confirm it's much more common to hear folks talking about how frustrating their school's schedules are:

- "There isn't enough time in the day for intervention."
- "We don't have enough staff to schedule all the electives we want to offer."
- "It's a shameful that some classes are mostly Black and Brown kids while others are overwhelmingly white."

Based on a few thousand conversations with folks from more than 250 districts across 30 U.S. states, we know that if you ask a teacher, principal, or central office leader what they like about their schedule, it's often a short list. When you ask what they *don't* like, the list is much longer. Our goal in writing this book is to change that. We want you to finish the book equipped with the tools and insights you need to design a schedule that's great for your kids, teachers, and budget. A schedule, in fact, that actually makes *you* want to shout, "I love our schedule!"

Why Focus on Scheduling?

The big idea that was the genesis of this book is as simple as it is far-reaching. Every school, every year, builds a master schedule. Clearly every school in the United States has someone who knows how to build a master schedule because more than 100,000 schools build one every year. And technically speaking, these schedules work: every student and every teacher has a place to be every hour of the school day.

So why do educators need a book on scheduling, then? This book is dedicated to shifting scheduling from a *technical* task, centered on making everything fit like Tetris blocks, to a *strategic* one: making a schedule that drives achievement, engagement, equity, and efficiency. A technical schedule focuses just on making sure every student and teacher knows where to be each period; a strategic schedule amplifies a district's priorities, encourages best practices in teaching and learning, heightens student engagement, ensures equity—and does all of this in a cost-effective manner.

We did not write this book as a technical scheduling guide or as one that provides instruction for how to use different scheduling software. If you are looking to learn the technical steps of building a basic schedule based on factors like the number of classrooms available, cafeteria capacity, and available staff, this is not the book for you. But if you are looking to learn what *should* be scheduled and how to overcome the common obstacles, both logistical and political, read on.

What Brought Us to Strategic Scheduling

They say confession is good for the soul, so Nate would like to come clean. For years, he never cared much about scheduling. It seemed less important than closing the achievement gap, accelerating learning, and increasing engagement. He was surprised to discover, however, that to do all those really exciting things, he needed to learn a lot about scheduling. Turns out, a great schedule is a means to an end, not an end itself.

When Nate was a superintendent, his leadership team mapped out a best-practice–based plan for dramatically improving outcomes, especially for students who struggled academically, and expanding course offerings in order to reengage many. The plan included uninterrupted core instruction, an end to pulling students from core reading and math to receive other services, providing extra time for intervention for all in need, grouping kids with similar needs together for extra help, having dedicated social-emotional learning (SEL) time twice a week, and offering electives aligned to students' interest and passion. When the district leadership team shared this plan with school leaders, they all said the same thing: "Great ideas, but the schedule won't let us do most off this." He learned in that moment that schedules can undermine the best of plans.

Over the next year, Nate and his leadership team created strategic schedules in each of the district's schools. Three years later, the high school had reduced the achievement gap by 40 points, and the elementary schools had reduced the number of struggling readers by two-thirds. Schedules had been an obstacle to achieving their plan, but they weren't an unsurmountable obstacle. More like an obstacle course that needed to be navigated.

David was much quicker to learn that a great schedule was a path to great achievement. As co-director of a middle school in Lawrence, Massachussetts, he saw firsthand how the restart of an underperforming middle school required much change, including a schedule change. When the schedule reinforced the turnaround plan, rather than hobbled it, the school became the fastest-improving public middle school in the state, as measured by student growth in math and English language arts (ELA).

Over the past combined 35 years, the two of us have helped hundreds of schools rethink how time is used during the day, and great things have followed for kids. We have also seen both the promise of strategic schedules and the pitfalls.

Snapshots of Success and Struggle

One large district in Georgia, for example, embraced elementary scheduling as a key lever for change. They had, perhaps for the first time, a deep conversation about schedule non-negotiables, defining what every child in the district deserved from their daily school experience. Eventually, the district leaders settled on very specific guarantees: each student would get 90 minutes of ELA, an hour of math, 30 minutes of daily intervention, and so on. They went further and mapped time blocks within these time blocks, what's known as *micro-scheduling*. This included, for example, stipulating that in grades K–2, the 90 minutes of ELA would include 20 minutes of phonics, a 5-minute daily check for understanding in math, and more. After rolling out the new schedules, good things started happening, among them a 30 percent increase in reading proficiency across 21 elementary schools in just 2 years. The superintendent went on to be the national superintendent of the year. Strategic schedules changed lives for the better in Bibb County Public Schools.

Unfortunately, not every scheduling story has a happy ending. We worked with a middle school where achievement was low, teachers disliked their schedule, and course offerings hadn't changed much since the era of VCRs. After a year of discussions, which created a very clear list of schedule changes that would be much better for kids and great for many teachers, the strategic scheduling effort hit a wall (well, actually a few walls). Yes, everyone agreed the schedule needed to include time for intervention and time to focus on the school's new SEL curriculum, but no teacher was willing to give up a minute of what was already in the schedule. Yes, their noncore offerings were outdated and unengaging, and yes, they knew what courses would excite their students, but a few teachers worried that the courses they were most comfortable teaching might get cut. And most upsetting, a staffing analysis (based on actual course enrollments and existing class-size guidelines) revealed that the school's math department should gain a full-time employee (FTE) and its world language department could lose one. This was met with immediate resistance. In the end, the middle school staff disliked the idea of change more than they disliked their schedule. Building strategic schedules takes more than just good intentions; it takes political acumen, the ability to generate a shared vision, and strong leadership.

When school and district leaders work together, get the facts, and create and pursue a vision based on best practices in teaching and learning, great things happen.

One mid-sized Ohio district embarked on a strategic scheduling process out of frustration. The central office was flummoxed by constant requests for more staff from principals in their middle and high schools. Principals were annoyed at the scheduling guidelines, procedures, and perceived interference from the central office. Students were angry that many of their first-choice electives were chronically overenrolled. Finally, teachers weren't happy that some staff taught fewer classes each day than others. But just six months down the line, a joint principal and central office team had not only removed nearly every friction point but also saved $2 million through attrition. The biggest surprise wasn't that all this friction could go away, but that they had never before attempted to address these long-simmering scheduling concerns. It seems too many schools just live with schedules they don't love.

The Pathway to Strategic Schedules

The details will be different in every school and every district, but all strategic schedules share common hallmarks. As shown in Figure 1.1, every strategic schedule has the following five elements:

1. **Strategies and priorities.** A school's or district's theory of action, students' needs, and culture should drive all the details of a strategic schedule.
2. **Time blocks.** How the school day is sliced into blocks of time can help or hinder the creation of schedules that align with best practices for teaching and learning.
3. **Course offerings.** The classes, courses, and subjects taught, and the levels of rigor at which they are taught, greatly affect a student's education.
4. **Staffing.** Having enough teachers (full-time, part-time, or shared) with the needed skills is central to creating a strategic schedule.
5. **Equity.** The first four elements on this list must be constantly examined and reexamined to ensure they are not deployed in ways that limit equitable access to opportunities and outcomes.

Let's unpack these five elements.

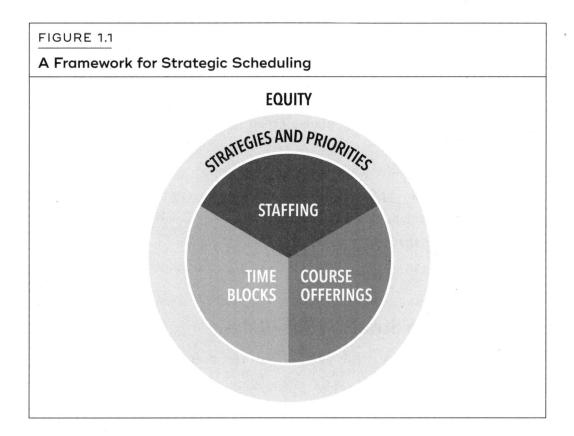

FIGURE 1.1

A Framework for Strategic Scheduling

Strategies and priorities

Too often folks try to build great schedules without first being very clear about the teaching, learning, and SEL strategies they want to use and the priorities for their school, based on the needs of their students. A master scheduler once shared, "You can schedule anything, just not everything." A failure to set clear priorities and establish some non-negotiables is the top reason schedules come up short.

Skipping or rushing through setting clear strategies and priorities often leads to an unhappy ending. For example, a suburban middle school asked us to help them revise their schedule. Like many other schools, they felt their current schedule was very problematic. No one was shouting, "I love our schedule!" at this school.

We shared that the first step in our work together was to align on key teaching and learning strategies and generate a short list of priorities. "No problem," they said. "We have a strategic plan."

Big problem, actually. Like so many strategic plans, the one in this district was too high-level and aspirational to inform schedule design in a useful way. To some staff, the goal that "all students will be college and career ready" meant there needed to be more honors classes; to others, this goal justified more intervention; and to others still, it meant there needed to be more career and technical education (CTE) offerings. Similarly, the school's goal to "meet the social-emotional needs of all students" was admirable but not clear. Did this mean that students should have an advisory period every day? That teachers should embed culturally relevant content into their lessons? As was the case in this school, it turns out that when folks fight over changing the schedule, they are mostly fighting over different priorities of what should be scheduled.

This particular suburban middle school decided it didn't have time to engage in a deep discussion of their priorities. Three years later, they still had the same schedule because they couldn't get agreement on a new one. All they could agree on was that nobody was happy.

In Chapter 2, we will share what research identifies as some of the most impactful scheduling-linked teaching and learning strategies for raising achievement, accelerating learning, and addressing social and emotional needs. This discussion can help schools agree on strategies and priorities that align to best practices and greatly influence schedule design.

Time blocks

How time in the day is sectioned tells how many minutes will be devoted to a subject, course, or activity. Mapping out the time blocks can be surprisingly frustrating. One elementary school we worked with illustrates why. This school seemed to have it all. Every day there were 90 minutes of reading; 30 minutes of intervention; an hour each for math, science, and social studies; and 40 minutes for art, music, and other "specials." There was also 10 minutes reserved daily for morning meeting and SEL blocks twice each week. Comprehensive, right? There was just one problem: all the blocks together totaled 460 minutes, and the school day was only 420 minutes long.

You'd be surprised how often this kind of "overbooking" occurs, and it's always because the leadership team didn't want to deprioritize any of these valuable uses of time. Yes, most schools could easily fill a longer day, but strategic schedules require prioritizing how limited and valuable minutes will be best used.

Another common form of wishful thinking is when middle and high schools declare they are adding intervention, advisory, or another elective by switching from a seven-period day to an eight-period day. This decision often feels like a victory. Something important got added and nothing was taken away! That's the usual thinking, anyway. In reality, every period got shorter. Losing 7.5 minutes per day of core subjects like math and ELA might not seem like a big deal, but it is equal to dropping 25 days of math and ELA instruction a year. Not quite the victory a school is typically looking for.

Strategic schedules treat every minute as precious, because every minute *is* precious. And they make sure the minutes mirror the priorities of the school and district.

Course offerings

It seems obvious, but before sitting down to design a schedule, it's crucial to have thought through what courses should be scheduled. Too often the course list is just rolled over from the prior year without anyone asking some important questions. Will you continue to offer lower-level remediation classes? (We hope not.) Are you going to have electives that align to student passions and interests? (We hope so.) Will you have intervention courses in math taught by math teachers? Will there be a class at the middle school to teach reading to kids who still struggle to read?

The key teaching and learning strategies and top priorities often become concrete only when they are reflected in course offerings (also known in some schools and districts as the *program of studies*). Although *course offerings* might sound like a secondary school term, elementary educators should also take note. Thinking of morning meeting, second step, social studies, intervention, and the like as course offerings helps structure the conversation about what should be included in an elementary master schedule.

A key lesson we've learned is that moving from a typical schedule to a strategic schedule more often involves changing what courses are offered than changing the number of periods in the day. Too much energy goes into debating "seven periods versus eight periods" and "block versus not block," while not enough is devoted to exploring what will be taught and how it will be taught during each period.

Staffing

When a principal, assistant principal, or guidance counselor looks up from the keyboard in frustration and says, "We just can't schedule everything we want," often the reason is not so much the lack of time but the lack of staff.

Most schedules are built around the staff a school has, which might seem obvious. Strategic scheduling turns this approach upside down. Rather than building a schedule based on the staff assigned to the school, strategic scheduling calculates the precise number of full-time employees (FTE) needed to build the schedule you want. If this sounds expensive and you are thinking about putting down the book because you are certain you won't be able to afford more staff, please keep reading.

After helping to design many hundreds of strategic schedules, we've found, to our surprise, that most schools don't need more staff to build the schedule they want—one that's great for kids, embeds best-practice teaching and learning strategies, and reflects key priorities. What these schools usually need is just a slightly different mix of staff. Chapter 9 delves into best practices for matching staffing to enrollment and presents a path to strategic schedules without adding FTE.

Another of the big surprises of strategic scheduling is realizing how often the time and talents of highly skilled staff don't have the reach and impact they could. Most school leaders feel their school is understaffed, but it's more often the case that their staff isn't scheduled optimally or has the wrong mix of skills for what the school hopes to achieve. If you are thinking, "Maybe this is true in some schools, but *we* don't have a *sliver* of extra capacity in our school!" be sure to read Chapter 9. As a preview, we'll share that in districts and schools that were 100 percent certain there were understaffed and fully optimized, we found

- A high school that could add six periods of math intervention, four periods of English intervention, and two reading support classes without adding staff.
- A mid-sized district that was able to save more than $2 million through attrition and reinvest the funds to expand both interventions and electives.
- A school that could add a half-dozen electives without adding a single FTE.

Staffing and budgeting are deeply interconnected, and strategic schedules manage both at the same time.

Equity

There are many aspects to improving equity, including ending disproportionate discipline, adding culturally responsive curriculum, and creating a climate that's welcoming to all. The master schedule and the first four elements of a strategic schedule are oft-overlooked levers for improving equity. To clarify, strategic scheduling can improve equity by

- Ensuring all students have access to high-rigor classes.
- Preventing situations in which less experienced teachers are disproportionately assigned to teach kids of color.
- Eliminating ineffective remedial classes disproportionately populated by kids of color, kids who are learning English, and kids with disabilities and replacing these classes with high-impact intervention.
- Guaranteeing all elementary students 100 percent of core reading and math instruction each day, with no pullout during these crucial time blocks.

An analytical review of current schedules through an equity lens can be enlightening. For example, one district learned that very few students of color were enrolled in honors social studies or English courses, yet plenty were enrolled—and doing well—in honors math and science courses. The leadership team was shocked when they saw the data. It wasn't overt racism that had created this terrible situation but unexamined differences in course entry requirements. The math and science departments used hard entrance criteria for placement, such as scores on end-of-semester exams and state test results. But because this approach was seen by many as rigid and inequitable, the English and social studies departments had incorporated seemingly more holistic criteria, such as teacher recommendation. Unfortunately, unconscious bias and a belief by some students that these courses "weren't for them" led to few kids of color in honors English and social studies.

Throughout this book, we will highlight ways strategic schedules can improve equity and point out common "potholes" to avoid. Chapter 8 also shares specific strategies to ensure equitable access to rigor at the high school level.

The Work Ahead

If you don't love your school's schedule, if you want higher achievement, more engaged students, and greater equity, then read on. If you want to have schedules that students, staff, and leaders feel meet their needs and do it cost effectively, or if you have struggled to overcome the pushback to changing a schedule, then read on. The chapters that follow will share practical advice, tips, and watch-out-fors. We have intentionally organized the book so that you can jump right to the sections most relevant to your school or district.

Here is a quick preview.

Best-practice research. In Chapter 2, we cover what research tells us about how a school's schedule can support or impede the implementation of best practices in teaching and learning and in student engagement. You might be surprised to learn that it doesn't really matter if you have a block schedule or not, but that trimming five minutes of phonics or 10 minutes of reading a day is a big deal. What matters in scheduling is well documented but not well understood. Many teachers and principals accept some "truths" as just that—but years of studies say otherwise.

Improving elementary schedules. In Chapters 3 and 4, we focus on strategic scheduling in elementary schools. At this level, you need both a detailed, thoughtful master schedule and interconnected schedules for special educators, interventionists, and related services. In an elementary school, it's not just one schedule in a school that matters but *many*. These two chapters lay out a step-by-step process for creating all the schedules in an elementary school in a strategic way.

Improving middle school schedules. In Chapters 5 and 6, attention shifts to middle school and how schedules at this level can best meet the needs of kids during these crucial transition years. Changing middle school schedules is hard, but it's worth the effort. You'll find practical strategies for meeting a wide range of academic needs and increasing student engagement (by a lot), all while staying faithful to the middle school model.

Improving high school schedules. Chapters 7, 8, and 9 cover strategic scheduling in high schools. High school schedules have long been debated and discussed, but new ways of providing intervention, increasing access to rigor, expanding electives without increasing costs, and matching staffing to course enrollment can convert a typical, just-OK high school schedule into an even better, strategic one. You'll find practical guidance for moving from good to great.

Improving the budget and scheduling process. The last two chapters of the book focus on issues relevant to leaders at all levels.

In Chapter 10, we look at how strategic schedules can help the budget as well as improve learning outcomes. In many ways, the schedule dictates the budget as much as the budget constrains the schedule. After analyzing hundreds of schools, it's clear to us that most schools can free up funds for redeploying staff through strategic scheduling. And equally important, many schools that think they need more staff to meet the needs of students find that what they really need is a better schedule.

Finally, in Chapter 11, we dig into the process for designing a strategic schedule. *Don't skip this chapter, please!* After a combined three-plus decades of wrestling with schedules, perhaps our most surprising finding has been that, in many schools and districts, the traditional *process* used to design and build the schedule and create the budget makes it nearly impossible to have strategic schedules. That process, which includes determining when the schedule is set, what the staffing needs are, and who will be included in the scheduling discussions each step of the way can unintentionally sabotage efforts to produce a strategic schedule. Read this chapter and learn how small changes to the process and timing of building schedules can help create the schedule you want.

This book is meant to be a practical guide to doing something familiar (the act of designing schedules) in a way that's more thoughtful and better for everyone. We hope to expose you to new and helpful approaches and ideas. We promise that, by the end of this book, you will think about schedules in a new way—as something as important to education outcomes and equity as your budget or your strategic plan.

2

What the Research Says About School Schedules

Best practices shared and myths busted

When we partner with educators across the United States to help them design and build strategic schedules, there is one question we are asked more often than any other: "What is the best type of schedule?" Unfortunately, they are asking the wrong question! As we will share in this chapter, it is the elements *within* the schedule that matter, and these best practices can fit inside many different models of schedules.

We have noticed that school and district leaders tend to overemphasize the schedule model and underappreciate the elements and components within the schedule itself. Certain schedule elements, such as ample time on core instruction and built-in extra time for academic intervention, are important in any schedule. In fact, research has identified seven best-practice principles that schools and districts should use to guide their scheduling efforts:

1. Spending more time on *high-quality* academic instruction results in more learning.
2. No one type of schedule model or period length is best.
3. Extra-time intervention helps struggling students catch up.
4. The time of day when subjects are taught does not matter much.

5. Providing students voice and choice increases engagement.

6. Students benefit from equitable access to rigor and high expectations—especially students from underserved populations.

7. Strategic scheduling is best accomplished as a team.

In this chapter, we examine each of these principles in more detail.

Principle 1: Spending More Time on *High-Quality* Academic Instruction Results in More Learning

It is unsurprising but nonetheless bears noting: the more time students spend receiving high-quality academic instruction taught by an effective teacher, the more they will learn (Aronson et al., 1998). If a student has math for 60 minutes day, for example, assuming high-quality academic instruction, effective curriculum, and other factors being equal, that student will learn more math than a student enrolled in a 50-minute-a-day class.

Strategic schedulers recognize this point and understand that even a small extension of class period length will add up over the course of a year. In a 180-day school year, for example, extending the elementary reading block by an additional 10 minutes—from 80 minutes to 90 minutes—adds the equivalent of *20 days* of reading instruction over the course of the year. Conversely, if a middle school were to move from, say, a seven-period day with 52-minute periods to an eight-period day with 44-minute periods, students in each course would lose the equivalent of *27 days* of instruction over the course of the year. Seemingly small changes in time spent on learning can make big differences for students!

So, more time equals more learning. Simple as that, right?

Mostly. Research has also made clear that longer classes or longer periods *do not in and of themselves make a difference*; what really matters is *how* the additional time is used. More school time produces more learning only when the time is focused on high-quality and productive academic activities (O'Brien, 2006). Said another way, how teachers use the instructional time they are allocated is more important than the length of the school day, the length of the class period, or the time of day that instruction occurs. In fact, researchers have concluded that there is little or no relationship between period length and student achievement—but a much larger relationship between *high-quality* instructional time and achievement (Aronson et al., 1998).

An example from David's time as a teacher highlights this point. Early in his career, he worked in a middle school as an 8th grade science teacher. One of David's outside-of-science teaching responsibilities was to supervise the 27 students in his homeroom during the drop-everything-and-read (DEAR) period that immediately followed homeroom. This 40-minute period was intended to provide more "literacy time" for students. Was this more time for reading than had been in the schedule previously? Most certainly. Was the time well used? Not exactly. Students who already read well usually did spend their DEAR time reading—sometimes books on or above grade level, and sometimes not. But students who struggled to read often did *not* read during the DEAR period, despite David's best efforts to convince and inspire them otherwise. Although David regularly incorporated what he understood to be effective literacy practices in his regular science instruction, he was not a trained literacy instructor. And even if he had been, the DEAR approach David's school adopted was essentially hands-off, asking students to read on their own without teacher intervention or guidance. As a result, this targeted literacy time had little impact on students who truly needed literacy support.

The types of time in a school day

Although spending more time on high-quality instruction matters, there is, of course, a lot more to school than reading, writing, and arithmetic. When you look at all the different activities students spend time on within a school day, it becomes clear that there are many important ways to use time; finding the right balance is key. One way to evaluate what you're doing now so that you can achieve that balance is by categorizing your schedule into five types of time (see Figure 2.1).

Here is a breakout of the categories:

- **Core instructional time:** Instructional time devoted to English language arts, math, science, and social studies.

FIGURE 2.1

The Five Types of Time with Examples

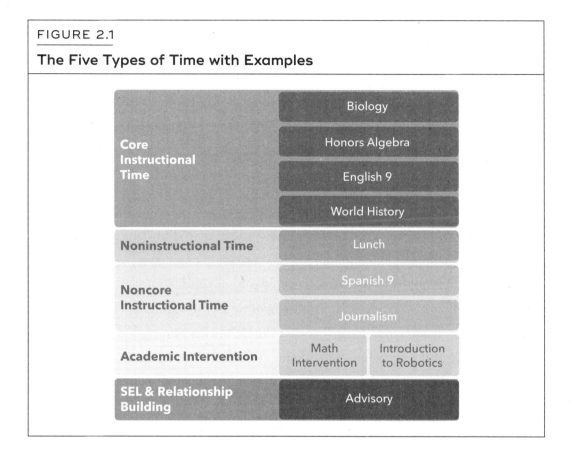

- **Noncore instructional time:** Instructional time devoted to electives and enrichment classes, or (at the elementary level) "specials"—unified arts or exploratory classes such as art, music, and physical education (PE).
- **Noninstructional time:** Time devoted to activities such as homeroom, lunch, and between-class transition.
- **Academic intervention:** Time devoted to providing targeted academic support to students, through content-specific intervention classes, What I Need (WIN) time, or "flex" blocks.
- **SEL- and relationship-building time:** Structured time devoted to developing students' social-emotional skills and time for students to build relationships with one another, their teachers, or other staff. Common examples include advisory, morning meeting, or community circle.

Schools can calculate the breakdown of time in their school by conducting a "use of time" study, which is as simple as examining a typical student's schedule, adding up the number of minutes devoted to each of the five categories of time, and then calculating the percentage of time devoted to each. Do this and you may be surprised at how time is allocated in your schedule. Many of the schools we have partnered with were.

Is there an optimal time balance?

The question for many school leaders at this point is "How much of the schedule *should* be devoted to each type of time?" Alas, there is no one right answer, but we have some suggestions.

Our own opinion on the best balance of school time is informed by personal experience building schedules; the hundreds of school schedules we have analyzed; and research we have reviewed on learning time, the importance of core academics, and the impact of the COVID-19 pandemic. Figure 2.2 shows what we think is the optimal time balance for core instruction for each grade level.

Some schools intentionally choose to spend less time on core instruction in order to provide more enrichment opportunities. Other schools actively choose

---

FIGURE 2.2

Typical Time Versus "Gold Standard" Time Spent on Core Instruction

Level	Hours of Core Instruction per Year	% of Total Time on Core Instruction	
		Typical	Gold Standard
Elementary	670–730	55–60%	55–60%
Middle	490–550	40–45%	50–55%
High	490–600	40–50%	50–55%

to spend more time on core instruction in order to bolster students' foundational skills. Both can work; the error is not knowing how time at your school is actually spent. And, as research points out, that balance of how time is allocated should ultimately be driven by your school's needs and priorities.

Principle 2: No One Type of Schedule Model or Period Length Is Best

Should you go with a six-period schedule or a seven-period one? Use a block schedule or trimester schedule? There is no shortage of schedule options for school and district leaders to choose from. Here are the most common options we see, each of which has both passionate fans and furious detractors:

- **Four-period A/B block schedule.** Students take four classes on "A-Day" and a separate set of four classes on "B-Day." Courses run for the full length of the school year, with exceptions for certain electives.

- **Five-period trimester schedule.** A trimester schedule divides the academic year into three sessions: fall, winter, and spring. Each trimester is approximately 12 to 13 weeks long. Students take approximately five classes per trimester, some of which run for multiple trimesters.

- **Six-period traditional schedule.** Students take six classes at the same time every day. Most classes run for the full length of the school year, though some electives may run for a quarter or semester.

- **Seven-period traditional schedule.** Students take seven classes at the same time every day. Most classes run for the full length of the school year, though some electives may run for a quarter or semester.

- **Eight-period traditional schedule.** Students take eight classes at the same time every day. Most classes run for the full length of the school year, though some electives may run for a quarter or semester.

We have seen each of these schedule types embrace best practices in teaching and learning and student engagement, but Figure 2.3 shows how significantly the

FIGURE 2.3

Hours of Instruction Per Year by Schedule Type

Schedule Type	Assumed Period Length	Hours per Year per Course
Eight-period	43 min	129
Four-period A/B block	90 min	135
Five-period with trimesters	72 min	144
Seven-period traditional	50 min	150
Six-period traditional	59 min	177

type of schedule a school uses can affect the amount of time devoted to core instruction. A six-period schedule (at 59 minutes per period), for example, would provide students 177 hours of math instruction per year, whereas an eight-period schedule (at 43 minutes per period) would provide just 129 hours.

Many districts have found that the seven-period schedule is a good balance. We have seen that it's easiest to fit the "gold standard" allocation of time into either the seven-period schedule or an A/B block schedule, especially if the block has a "skinny period" (more on that in Chapter 7).

The impact on teachers

Looking at schedules strictly from the vantage point of minutes per day and allocation across different uses of time fails to consider a critical factor: how it affects teachers.

The cost on teacher morale associated with switching schedule models can be significant. Even in schools where staff do not like the existing model, switching schedules can nosedive teacher satisfaction, if not effectiveness, because it forces them to change lesson plans and teaching styles. Consider, for example, that moving from an eight-period schedule to an A/B block does not mean a teacher can simply take a pair of 45-minute lesson plans and staple them together for a 90-minute period that meets every other day. A teacher may be accustomed to using the gradual release of responsibility lesson structure ("I do it alone/We do it together/ You do it alone") in a 45-minute period; switching to a 90-minute period would require them to find new ways to extend and structure the lesson's "You do it alone" portion (independent practice). It would mean creating new lessons with different activities, pacing, and structures. In our work with districts, we have seen that when schools switch schedule models and teachers opt to stick with their old style and plans, learning and engagement tend to decline.

David has lived through a schedule model switch, and it was not easy. Early in his career, when he taught 8th grade science in 90-minute A/B block periods, he had ample time to facilitate extended lab activities within the confines of a single class. At the same time, he sometimes struggled to fill the full 90 minutes, usually because students moved through lesson activities more quickly than expected. Two years later, he switched schools and taught 6th grade science in 60-minute periods. This required significant adjustments to his curriculum and lesson plans, such as splitting labs over the course of two periods, which also meant losing additional cleanup and transition time. Even with the help of an incredible instructional coach and a talented fellow 6th grade science teacher, it took David nearly two full years to successfully adjust from an A/B block schedule to a six-period schedule.

Nate saw the challenge of switching schedules through the eyes of a great math teacher who loved math and teaching math; both her AP Calculus and intervention students outperformed all others in the district and across the state. When this teacher's school decided to move from a seven-period schedule to a block schedule, she opted to retire five years early rather than redesign all her lessons.

So, should you *never* switch schedule models? Of course not. But first you must carefully consider what improvements your school is looking to make. If it's possible to achieve those improvements by adjusting certain elements of the current schedule instead of switching the entire schedule model, this is usually the better path.

The challenge of the "semester" block schedule

Though the trend at the high school level over the past two decades has been to shift to a block schedule model, a meta-analysis of 58 empirical studies of high school block schedules indicated that block scheduling, at least as it has been commonly implemented, has little practical or consistent ability to significantly improve student performance in and of itself (Zepeda & Mayers, 2006). Overall, research has shown that students in block and nonblock scheduled schools have equivalent end-of-course test scores (Rettig & Canady, 1999).

If you are set on using a block schedule, should you use an A/B block or a 4×4 semester block (see Figure 2.4)? In the latter model, students take four 90-minute classes every day during the first semester and a different set of four 90-minute classes every day during the second semester.

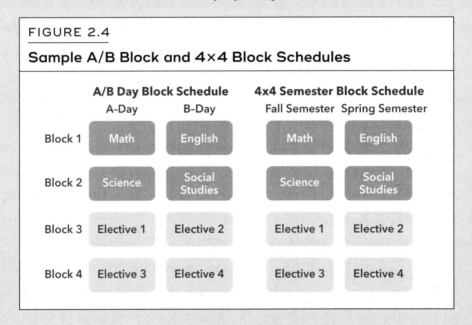

FIGURE 2.4

Sample A/B Block and 4×4 Block Schedules

| | **A/B Day Block Schedule** | | **4x4 Semester Block Schedule** | |
	A-Day	B-Day	Fall Semester	Spring Semester
Block 1	Math	English	Math	English
Block 2	Science	Social Studies	Science	Social Studies
Block 3	Elective 1	Elective 2	Elective 1	Elective 2
Block 4	Elective 3	Elective 4	Elective 3	Elective 4

Here are a few things to consider. The 4×4 semester block schedule can be especially challenging for students who struggle. There are two likely reasons. First, if they take math at the beginning of the school year, they have a gap of 10–15 weeks from their last math class to the state test in math. Even students who do well in class can forget a lot over 10–15 weeks. Second, students who struggle benefit from extra-time intervention that is delivered throughout the school year. Districts we have partnered with consistently report that the A/B block schedule is easier to implement, easier to manage, provides more consistent support for students who struggle, and has less political pushback than the 4×4 semester block schedule.

The need for PD

Ultimately, professional development (PD) and support is key to the successful implementation of any schedule model. School and district leaders need to have a clear vision for the new schedule, communicate why it's needed to teachers and staff, and provide educators a variety of supports (e.g., training sessions, coaching, group lesson-planning opportunities, lesson study) to help them transition their lesson plans and teaching style. Research (e.g., Farbman & Kaplan, 2005; Irmsher, 1996) concludes that adequate teacher development focused on modifying instructional strategies and lessons is the determining factor in whether students will achieve better or worse under a new scheduling model—not the scheduling model itself.

The student adaptability factor

Whatever schedule model is chosen, one thing is consistently clear: students tend to handle complex schedules more easily than teachers, administrators, and parents. Here's testimony to that effect from a high school principal we work with—someone who runs a complex rotating drop schedule in which students are enrolled in eight courses but take only six on any given day:

> At the beginning of the school year, I meet with parents and discuss the schedule. After I explain how it works, I usually say, "You're probably confused—that's fine and expected. Your student will know their schedule inside and out, and that's all you need to know."

Principle 3: Extra-Time Intervention Helps Struggling Students Catch Up

Research has made it clear that students with significant or persistent learning challenges do better when they have multiple opportunities to practice a skill or strategy (Gersten et al., 2009). If fact, some students require 10–30 times more opportunities to practice than their peers to effectively apply a skill or strategy.

Regular class time, even in a block schedule, does not provide enough time for many students to master the skills and content necessary to be successful. This is especially true for knowledge and skills in foundational subjects like math, reading, and writing, which are necessary for nearly every other type of course at every grade level. Science, social studies, and world languages are difficult to master without strong literacy skills, for example. Research has also clarified that any answer to catching up kids who are academically behind should include building in extra-time intervention in the form of What I Need (WIN) intervention blocks at the elementary level and content-specific intervention courses at the secondary level (Grossman, 2021).

At elementary schools, extra-time learning opportunities can take the form of either an intervention and enrichment block (usually 30–45 minutes a day) or an extended learning block for specific subjects like math or reading. For example, an elementary school might consider extending its 90-minute literacy block to 120 minutes to allow for 30 minutes of intervention for additional, beyond-the-core, small-group instruction.

At the secondary level, extra-time supports should include either content-specific intervention courses, such as a math foundations course that is built into a student's schedule in addition to grade-level core instruction, or the creation of a highly structured common intervention block in which students can receive targeted academic support *or* access to an additional enrichment elective. Note that we did not call the intervention a "flex block" or WIN period—such terms at the secondary level, we find, are often code for "study hall." If you choose to incorporate a common intervention block into the schedule, it needs to be just that: a well-structured period devoted to providing academic intervention to students who have skill and content gaps *and* providing ample and structured enrichment activities for students who do not need intervention.

During the extra-time intervention, a content-strong teacher should offer need-based, just-in-time academic supports that help address students' misconceptions about or challenges with both current-year and prior-year content. Instruction provided during extra-time intervention should be direct instruction that's targeted to identified skill needs and misunderstandings.

A common misconception about providing academic supports to students who struggle is that co-teaching or push-in support are "equal" alternatives to extra-time intervention. This is not true, as neither of these options gives students *actual extra time* to master content from prior years, nor does it give teachers the time they need to address student skill gaps.

The question you might be asking at this point is "This is all well and good, but where do I find the time in the school schedule—let alone the staff—for extra-time learning and intervention opportunities for students?" See Chapters 3, 5, and 8 for specific suggestions and strategies for effectively incorporating extra-time intervention into your school schedule.

Principle 4: The Time of Day When Subjects Are Taught Does Not Matter Much

The question the "optimal" time of day to teach certain subjects arises frequently in our work, especially in elementary schools. As one elementary principal told us, "We always make sure to schedule math in the morning. The students are more awake then and respond better to math instruction."

This "morning is better" thinking is very deeply rooted with many elementary teachers and principals. Although research confirms that not all times of the school day are created equal, when it comes to student learning, the time of day when instruction occurs does play some part in achievement for some students (Pope, 2016). Here is the more important point, though: compared to other factors—such as the skill of the teacher teaching, the quality of the curriculum, and the engagement of the students—when a subject is taught during the school day is a much less important variable (Marzano, 2003). Much of the research suggests that educators would be wise to take a more nuanced approach to the question about the best time of day for learning beyond "morning is better than afternoon." Not all students perform better in the morning than the afternoon, and research is inconclusive as to whether there is an optimal time to offer particular subjects.

Principals we have worked with have been surprised to learn that stacking reading and math in the morning in an elementary master schedule can limit the impact of intervention staff and hurt students with IEPs. Here is how we've seen that scenario play out: An elementary school schedules all the math blocks and most of the reading blocks for all grades in the morning because "students learn better in the morning." This means that about half the students who get pullout services (e.g., speech and language or reading support from a special educator) must be pulled out from core reading and math instruction. A school that tries to avoid this by stacking intervention periods in the afternoon winds up limiting the number of students the school's math and reading interventionists can serve.

There is one notable exception to the research finding that the time of day when subjects are taught matters less than people think: start times at secondary schools. Adolescents typically have a preference to stay active later in the evening and wake up later in the morning (Dunster et al., 2018). Even the most experienced and talented teachers can find it challenging to combat adolescents' unique circadian rhythms. In 2014, the American Academy of Pediatrics went so far as to issue a policy statement urging middle and high schools to adjust start times to no earlier than 8:30 a.m. to aid students in getting sufficient sleep to improve their overall health. As of 2015, the average start time across secondary schools in the country was 8:03 a.m., with secondary schools in Louisiana averaging the earliest school start time of 7:40 a.m. (Wheaton et al., 2015).

Some districts have adjusted to this reality and have pushed start times back at their secondary schools. Seattle Public Schools, for example, decided to delay secondary school start time from 7:50 to 8:45 a.m. starting in 2016. The result was significantly fewer tardies and absences (Dunster et al., 2018). A 2021 study from the University of Minnesota documented four districts in Minnesota that postponed the start of the school day by 20–65 minutes for 18,000 students in 5th grade through 11th grade. It concluded that the later start times resulted in students being 16 percent more likely to get the recommended hours of sleep (Barshay, 2021).

Despite the documented benefits, taking steps to push back start times takes careful planning and can be politically challenging. Yes, it is hard to change middle and high school start times, especially because pushing back the first bell means fewer daylight hours for after-school sports. Changes to elementary start times can result in bus-routing issues and complexities with childcare providers. These are just a few of the many reasons parents and staff often resist later start times.

Perhaps the worst change to start times is the purely symbolic one—those incremental shifts districts may adopt as a "keep the peace" compromise or a "something is better than nothing" solution. For example, one district we worked with spent three years studying high school start time adjustment and ultimately decided to move the start of the day back by 10 minutes—from 8:00 a.m. to 8:10. With traffic, the resulting schedule lengthened many students' morning bus rides by more than 15 minutes. These students had to get up earlier, and the 10 minutes was not enough time to help any student in a meaningful way.

Principle 5: Providing Students Voice and Choice in Scheduling Increases Engagement

Nearly all schools are striving to improve student engagement. The most common strategy is to find dedicated time in the schedule for relationship building, but engagement can also be improved by giving students more control over what's in their schedule. This is especially relevant for middle school students, who often want more voice and choice than they are traditionally offered. (See Chapter 6 for more on this.)

A few definitions to start. *Student choice,* as part of scheduling, means providing students with the opportunity to choose from a set of course options. *Student voice,* by comparison, is about giving students opportunities to inform what those course options are. A significant amount of research has shown that the more schools give students of all ages voice and choice, the more motivation and engagement are likely to rise (Zeiser et al., 2018). Enhanced student agency has been linked to a variety of important education outcomes, including elevated achievement levels in historically marginalized student populations, greater classroom participation and engagement, and decreases in behavioral problems. Increasing student voice is particularly important for historically marginalized populations, including students from Latinx, Black, Native American, and low-income communities, as well as students with disabilities (Benner et al., 2019).

These findings highlight two important considerations for those looking to provide students with opportunities for more voice and choice. First, students should not be allowed to opt out of key academic activities, such as academic intervention. Voice and choice should not prevent students from receiving needed academic supports. Second, schools and districts need to determine what level of voice and choice they would like to offer students. Imagine a continuum of voice and choice: on the far left is complete student voice and choice, on the far right is zero student voice and choice. Though research is limited as to what the "right" balance of student voice and choice is, schools and districts should consider varying student voice and choice across grade levels and explicitly name the degree of voice and choice that students can expect.

Principle 6: Students Benefit from Equitable Access to Rigor and High Expectations—Especially Students from Underserved Populations

We have found that both confident, experienced schedulers and novice ones recognize that a school's schedule is the primary driver of how a school's resources—time, staff, space—are allocated and managed. They know that a schedule dictates foundational elements of the student experience, including which teachers and classmates will work together; the size, composition, and timing of classes; access to academic supports; and access to rigorous and engaging courses. The best schedulers manage to navigate all the logistical hurdles of building a schedule *while also* being mindful of the ways in which scheduling decisions can create unintended inequities.

A 2021 white paper from the Center for Public Research and Leadership at Columbia University summarizes this challenge well:

The complex and detailed nature of master schedules mean they are often over-looked as core to a district's and school's strategy. It is easy to get lost in the details of master scheduling without thinking about the choices that drive the scheduling process. They appear like operational choices at first—offer English 1st period, schedule in 90-minute blocks—but they can have wide-reaching consequences on students' access to opportunity and overall quality of learning. In particular, focusing on the details but not their effect often leads to reduced access and opportunity for the most marginalized, including Latino students, Black students, students experiencing poverty, students with disabilities, and multilingual learners. (Clay et al., p. 1)

One of the most widespread scheduling-induced inequities is access to rigorous courses and effective teachers at the high school level. An unfortunately common example is when a school's enrollment policies disproportionately exclude students, especially students of color, from advanced courses like honors, advanced placement (AP), and International Baccalaureate (IB) classes. Common roadblocks to equitable course enrollment include

- Prerequisites that have limited relevance to students' actual likelihood of success.
- Reliance on teacher recommendations that are shaped by bias—conscious or not.
- Excluding academically able students due to discipline or attendance history, neither of which predicts a student's ability to master high-level material.
- Grade point averages lowered by policies that factor in homework completion.
- Belief that access to honors or AP/IB courses should inherently be limited.
- Tracking—the automatic enrollment of students who have taken honors or AP/IB courses in previous years or semesters and the automatic exclusion of those who haven't.

A different common example of inequitable scheduling practices is when veteran teachers "earn the right" to teach honors or AP courses (where students are presumed to be more capable and more engaged) and avoid teaching general, introductory, or intervention courses (where students are presumed to be less engaged or more challenging). A strategic schedule flips this pattern on its head, assigning the most experienced, most effective teachers (including the department head) to teach general, introductory, and intervention courses. Schools that have accomplished this have done so through a combination of status, incentives, and expectations. All middle school and high school math teachers in one district, for example, were required to teach one section of math intervention (though this varied slightly based on actual student need) each year. Schedules were created and schools were staffed with the assumption that teachers would teach four sections of math and one section of math intervention.

Another district made it known that future high school department heads would be drawn only from staff that effectively taught intervention, another gave first priority for grant-funded professional development opportunities to intervention staff. Perhaps most impactful of all, a few districts we have worked with made it explicit that only the most effective staff would be asked to teach intervention. In these districts, it was a badge of honor to teach students who struggle, and teachers vied for the privilege.

Research points the way forward when it comes to providing equitable access to high-rigor courses. For example, researchers at the Center for Public Research and Leadership at Columbia University (Clay et al., 2021) recommend schools and districts regularly assess student access to rigor by asking questions like these:

- What rigorous courses are available to students?
- Which students actually enroll in rigorous courses?
- Which students are succeeding in rigorous courses?
- What supports can we provide to help more students succeed in rigorous courses?

We explore these questions and other questions about equity and rigor (specifically at the high school level) in Chapter 8.

Principle 7: Strategic Scheduling Is Best Accomplished as a Team

Designing and building a schedule that serves students well, is good for teachers and other staff, and is financially feasible is no easy task. First, there is the challenge of identifying *what* to schedule. Second, there is the technical challenge of *how* to actually build the master schedule. Both are easier when the right people are in the room. Here is what our work and the research has taught us about using teamwork to address both challenges.

Despite its deep and wide-ranging impact on students and staff, scheduling is too often done in a vacuum—handled by one person or a very small group of people who seldom involve those outside the group. Does this approach result in a schedule? Sure. We have never visited a school *without* some kind of schedule, however imperfect. But does this approach lead to the best possible schedule that students and staff understand, appreciate, and are invested in? Unlikely.

A large, complex task like scheduling is best approached as a team sport. Bringing in multiple perspectives—to generate ideas and offer feedback—increases the odds of producing a schedule that will work for as many students and staff as possible, not just those who are easiest to schedule for. It also helps ensure that *what* is scheduled aligns with the school's overall goals and priorities. Additionally, a team approach can increase staff investment in the schedule outcomes.

As for the technical challenge of creating a schedule, anyone who has ever done it knows that it's a skill that some have developed more than others. When assembling your scheduling team, it is important to assess with clear eyes who has scheduling expertise. *Without* an expert scheduler, you can expect two things to happen: (1) the schedule will take a long time to build, and (2) the schedule will be less than ideal and will not fully reflect the school's priorities.

In Chapter 11, we provide suggestions on how to approach scheduling as a team and leverage the expertise of a skilled scheduler.

◆ ◆ ◆

The good news is that research maps a path from technical schedules to strategic schedules—from schedules that meet the minimum requirements to ones that raise achievement, improve engagement, and address inequities. These research-based, best-practice-centered recommendations hold true for all grade levels—elementary, middle, and high school—but they need to be applied a bit differently at each level. Read on to learn how you can improve your school's schedule based on this best-practice research.

Elementary School

3

Making Elementary Master Schedules More Strategic

A new look at some well-established practices

Every elementary school, every year, builds a new master schedule, and all these schedules "work fine." By that, we mean these schedules ensure that every student gets lunch and the cafeteria isn't overloaded; that art, music, PE, and other specials fit into the school week; and that classroom teachers have a good idea of how much time to spend on morning meeting, reading, and so on. A master schedule that "works fine" covers all these bases. But what it can't do—and what a strategic master schedule *can*—is lead to dramatic gains in student achievement and improve equity.

Bibb County Public Schools in Georgia has shown what's possible with strategic scheduling. The district has 21 elementary schools, and few of these schools' principals had concerns about their master schedule. The schedules were fine—not great, but not a glaring problem either. What *was* a problem in Bibb County's elementary schools was low reading achievement and unacceptable outcomes for historically underserved students. Superintendent Curtis Jones Jr. learned about strategic scheduling and was hopeful, if uncertain, that better elementary schedules could lead to better outcomes. Most of the district's principals were dubious.

A review of elementary master schedules across Bibb County Public Schools showed wide variation in what was scheduled and how time was used. History and preference seemed to explain these differences. With a careful planning process, clear priorities, thoughtful non-negotiables, the adoption of micro-schedules, and an infusion of expert schedulers, Bibb County embraced strategic scheduling, and learning in the district's elementary schools skyrocketed. Over the next few years, reading proficiency for the 3rd grade cohort increased by 15 percentage points, and the superintendent was named 2019 National Superintendent of the Year by the School Superintendents Association (Corley, 2022).

Leaders in both the central office and in the schools, a bit to their surprise, came to realize that master schedules could accelerate learning—be strategically important and not just "work fine." They learned that master schedules could either encourage or undermine teaching and learning best practices, and to achieve the former, they needed a short list of priorities, a lot of collaboration between school leaders and the central office, and additional scheduling expertise.

Continue reading this chapter to learn how Bibb County and other districts have raised student achievement through strategic elementary schedules and how you can apply these approaches to build a strategic master schedule in your elementary school or in the elementary schools throughout your district. Details on school/central office teamwork and where to find scheduling expertise are discussed in Chapter 11.

Start by Looking to Teaching and Learning Best Practices

Schedules are a means to an end, not an end in and of itself. Having clarity on what works in teaching and learning is the first step to building a great schedule. These are the strategies and priorities referenced in our framework in Chapter 1. Experienced schedulers like to say you can schedule anything, just not everything. Before building a schedule, it's crucial to state and agree on the schedule's top priorities.

The work of researcher John Hattie (2008), the What Works Clearinghouse (Gersten et al., 2008), the National Reading Panel (National Institute of Child Health and Human Development, 2000), and the experience of schools that have successfully closed their achievement gap helps to identify the seven best practices that should drive the development of elementary master schedules:

- Provide 90 minutes of reading and 60 minutes of math daily.
- Schedule dedicated time for writing.
- Prioritize reading, writing, math, SEL, and interventions.
- Provide 30 minutes a day of reading intervention for all students who struggle to read.
- Follow a detailed micro-schedule within the reading block.
- Stagger grade-level reading, math, and intervention (and enrichment) blocks.
- Provide grade-level common planning time.

Yes, these teaching and learning best practices are deeply intertwined with elementary schedules. But how these blocks of time are laid out in the master schedule influences whether these best practices can come to life. Let's take a closer look at each of these best practices and how strategic scheduling can support them.

Scheduling Daily Reading and Math Blocks

The research is clear that elementary students need at least 90 minutes of reading (Underwood, 2018) and 60 minutes of math every day (Louisiana Department of Education, 2021). It's easy enough to state this before you design a schedule, but it can be tricky to actually reserve this time for reading and math blocks when you start to layer in all the other desired subjects and activities. For this reason, there is great value in writing down how the blocks of time during the day should be used—that is, exactly how many minutes are devoted to each subject and activity throughout the day. This gets at the blocks-of-time component of the strategic scheduling framework. It's a step that might seem obvious, but after helping more than 500 elementary schools build their schedule, we find it is often skipped or abandoned without reaching agreement.

There is a dirty little secret we want to share—not to be mean but to start a tough, honest conversation. There is so much to do each day and so little time to do it. (That's not the secret.) The secret is that in too many schools and districts, central office leaders ask principals to schedule more than can possibly fit in a day, and principals pass this unrealistic burden on to their teachers. For an example from a district we supported, see Figure 3.1, which is a summary of a memo issued by the central office articulating a clear set of scheduling expectations for all principals.

"What do you think of this list?" a principal asked us. We reviewed it and replied that we thought it well conceived. When the principal pushed back, we interpreted his anger as typical resistance to change. Then another principal advised us to grab a calculator and add up the minutes. To our surprise, the "well-conceived" schedule totaled 460 minutes . . . which was 40 minutes longer than the school day. On closer inspection, we saw that the expectations also included a brief morning meeting but no time for the district's newly rolled-out SEL program.

In a similar vein, we had a principal share with pride a newly finalized master schedule that purportedly "covered all the bases" but was actually longer than the school day and still didn't include time for an explicitly stated school priority. It's not

---

FIGURE 3.1

Sample District-Issued Scheduling Expectations

Schedule Component	Duration in Minutes
Morning meeting	15
Reading	120
Math	60
Specials	40
Lunch	30
Recess	25
Writing	30
Spanish	10
Science	45
Social studies	45
Intervention (WIN time)	40

that the leaders who create these schedules struggle with being able to add up the minutes in a day or the minutes in the schedule so much as they struggle to make hard tradeoffs. Strategic schedules are realistic and never ask for more than what's possible.

Before starting to build an elementary mastery schedule, make a simple chart like the one in Figure 3.1 for each grade level. List every time block you want to schedule, and don't forget writing instruction, SEL, morning meeting, or anything else that requires dedicated time. Next, list how many minutes you'll allot for each block. Finally, add up all the minutes and compare that sum to the length of the official school day. The chart you just created should serve as the basis of your "What should we schedule?" conversation and can ensure that you protect 90 minutes of reading and 60 minutes of math in every day's schedule.

Providing Dedicated Time for Writing

Nate remembers asking a group of teachers if writing was supposed to be taught as *part* of the 90-minute reading block listed in their school schedule or *in addition* to it. There was no consensus, even though the schedule had been in place for three years. Within the same district, and even within the same school, some teachers said, "Yes, writing is definitely part of the 90 minutes," while others said, "No, writing is taught separately; it gets its own 30 minutes, three times a week." One teacher, who had been teaching in the same school, at the same grade level, and with the same materials for four years, admitted that she wasn't sure. "I keep wondering," she said, "and I wish someone would answer this question."

To be crystal clear: make time to learn writing its own priority, and give it space the schedule in addition to the 90 minutes reserved for reading.

Prioritizing Reading, Writing, Math, SEL, and Interventions

Before music teachers, social studies directors, and others object, yes, there is more to a balanced education than just ELA, math, SEL, and interventions. We would never say that subjects like foreign language, art, and science or activities like recess are unimportant . . . just that they are *second* most important. The distinction is significant. Being second most important means that students should definitely receive high-quality instruction in these subjects, get recess, and eat lunch, but when designing a master schedule, tradeoffs are necessary, and the priorities must be clear and honored.

After interviewing hundreds of elementary principals and assistant principals, we see an odd disconnect between stated and actual priorities. Nearly all say reading and math are vital; however, specials and lunch seem to overrule all else when it's time to build the master schedule. Here is a typical comment:

> We had to split the reading block into three disconnected chunks to accommodate the art and music teachers' schedules, and we only do 45 minutes of math each day. There just isn't enough time for everything.

Similarly, while school leaders generally proclaim the importance of SEL, many don't carve out dedicated time in the schedule for it; instead, they ask teachers to "weave it in" whenever possible, despite knowing that the curriculum is already packed full. "Weave it in" doesn't sound like an effective way to address a top priority.

For sure, SEL can and should be embedded in other subjects and be part and parcel of how teachers manage their classrooms and interact with students. But some schools, many in fact, also purchase scripted SEL programs that require dedicated time to teach. While working with a group of 250-plus elementary educators from roughly 30 districts, Nate asked them to raise their hand if their school had a purchased SEL program that had specific lessons to teach. Nearly every hand went up. Then he asked them to keep their hand up if time for these lessons was listed in the master schedule. All but a few hands came down. Finally, Nate asked them to keep their hand up if they had provided or received guidance on what to stop teaching in order to make room for the new SEL material. Not a single hand was left in the air. All these schools prioritized SEL, but none had been willing to specify what had to be a second priority to make room for it.

Ensuring 30 Minutes of Daily Reading Intervention for Those Who Struggle

Even before the disruption of the COVID-19 pandemic, far too many elementary-age students struggled to read. These students need more than 90 minutes a day of reading instruction; they also need at least 30 minutes a day of reading intervention delivered by a skilled reading teacher (Gersten et al., 2008).

Based on our review of thousands of elementary schedules, we would say that only about half the elementary schools in the country have dedicated extra time for reading intervention in their master schedule, and some of them offer intervention only a few times a week. The other half aren't saying intervention isn't important; they simply point out that there is no time in the day for it.

Arlington Public Schools in Massachusetts provides an example of a district that faced this challenge by launching a planning process with principals and the central office to set scheduling priorities. Providing 30 minutes of daily reading intervention for struggling readers was near the top of their list, put there with little debate and lots of head nodding. However, a few months later, when the principals finished their master schedules, only one of the district's seven elementary schools had a daily intervention block. Why the backtracking? The six principals explained they just couldn't fit it in without lengthening the day—which, of course, was impractical and unrealistic. So how did the one school manage fit an intervention block into the standard school day? The principal explained their process:

> Since we needed to free up 30 minutes for intervention (and enrichment for those who didn't struggle), something already in the schedule had to come out. We realized that the daily block of time that had been dedicated to teaching social studies was mostly reading and writing about history and other cultures. Well, reading and writing isn't just social studies—it's ELA too. We mapped the social studies curriculum and merged it into the ELA curriculum. Half of the independent reading books in the classroom library were aligned to the social studies content (and available at different reading levels), and half the ELA writing

assignments and book reports were also directly connected to the social studies standards. By having ELA also cover the social studies content, we made time for intervention.

Even the district's K–12 social studies director strongly embraced this plan. She commented, "I want all kids to be able to take AP History in high school, which means they need to be able to read and comprehend well in the elementary grades."

This solution is not the only way to provide daily intervention, but it highlights the difference between looking for time to include a "would-be-nice-to-have" and making time for a top priority. Some elementary schools alternate science and social studies every other day (especially in K–2), and others shorten lunch, recess, and specials a bit to find the needed 30 minutes for daily intervention. Others still opt for approaches that may *seem* like a solution but often fall short.

For example, a far too common approach to finding time for intervention is to offer it before or after school. "It's the perfect solution!" is a common refrain. Well, it's perfect if intervention is the lowest priority—something that's optional and low-impact rather than critical for preventing negative long-term consequences. Before- and after-school intervention is also the perfect solution if your top priority is not upsetting teachers and staff who might feel insulted that their time block was cut back or integrated elsewhere in the schedule. Before- and after-school intervention doesn't rock the boat, but it does throw a lot of students out of the boat—particularly those from historically underserved populations and poor families. Think of how many students don't have transportation options that allow them to come to school early or stay late. Think of how many students have family obligations or activities that would keep them out of optional intervention held outside the standard school day, and of how many will just opt out—because how urgent could something be if it's offered but not required?

Access to quality intervention is a clear example of how equity and scheduling interconnect. Before- and after-school intervention is an inequitable and insufficient approach to the problem of a too-crowded school day. Schedule creators can and must do better.

Creating a Detailed Micro-Schedule for the Reading Block

A reading block is prominent on nearly all elementary master schedules. This big chunk of time—90 or 120 minutes or more—proclaims the importance of reading. This is good, but it's not enough. Within one school, and within one grade level even, there can be wildly inconsistent uses of a 90-minute reading block. One 1st grade teacher might devote 20 minutes of that daily block to phonics instruction, another might devote 10 minutes a day to phonics, and a third might spend just 5 minutes on phonics twice a week. What if some 2nd grade teachers dedicate half of every 90-minute reading block to independent reading while others use those 45 minutes for small-group instruction? All these teachers are honoring the 90 minutes scheduled for reading, yet they all spend the time in different ways, and students will feel the effects. Here again, schedules and equity interconnect. Every student is entitled to receive best-practice instruction—including direct instruction in phonics and all the elements of a research-based reading curriculum.

This is why strategic elementary master schedules include a micro-schedule for the reading block. It's a way to guide teachers toward, and ensure universal access to, best practices. Some schools create a micro-schedule for the math block as well.

The experience of Moundsview Public Schools in Minnesota highlights the power of micro-schedules. The district spent a year piloting research-based curriculum before settling on a widely used, high-quality curriculum. Teachers, principals, and central office leaders felt good about the choice. Over the next few years, Moundsview invested heavily in professional development, common planning time, and instructional coaching to roll out the new curriculum. Everything seemed and felt good, yet after three years, reading achievement scores hadn't budged. Sadly, they were prepared to select a different curriculum because their first choice was clearly a bust.

Nate was asked to help review an alternative curriculum, yet he couldn't find meaningful differences between it and the one the district had spent three years rolling out. The current program was well respected and thoughtfully aligned to the science of reading. He asked to see the elementary master schedules and teaching materials. As expected, each school's schedule included a big green block labeled "Reading," but there were no details.

In focus groups, more than 100 Moundsview teachers shared that they liked the curriculum and followed it closely. When pressed for details, however, these teachers struggled to say exactly how they sliced and diced the 90 minutes reserved for reading instruction. How much time did they spend on phonics, whole-class read-alouds, small-group support, independent reading, writing, and vocabulary? Responses included "it depends," "it varies by day," and "I base it on how the students are doing that day." No one had a specific answer measured in minutes. A handful of candid souls shared, "The reading curriculum is a lot to fit into 90 minutes; many days I can't do everything I know I should."

With so much ambiguity, Nate suggested a week-long detailed time study. The results explained everything. Some teachers, grades, or whole schools spent very little time teaching phonics, a few spent so much time on phonics they had to skip small-group instruction some days, and more than a few teachers spent almost the entire 90 minutes on whole-class instruction or independent reading. Three key truths emerged:

- Teachers wanted to follow the curriculum.
- No one had ever translated the curriculum's hundreds of pages of materials and lessons into clear time allocations.
- Absent official guidance, most teachers created their own ad hoc micro-schedule, often unconsciously and seldom in writing.

Unfortunately, very few teachers in Moundsview elementary schools were actually implementing all the parts and pieces of the reading curriculum. Newer teachers especially struggled with covering all the expectations in 90 minutes.

With this time study, and working with groups of teachers, a central office reading director, and recommendations from the central office curriculum developer,

Moundsview Public Schools went on to create very specific time allocations for each aspect of teaching reading. These micro-schedules differed by grade, but not by school or teacher. Thanks to greater clarity on how to use the time within the reading block, teachers were able to implement the curriculum with fidelity, and the number of struggling readers dropped by a third in the next year. Even bigger gains followed.

The sample in Figure 3.2 is just that—a sample. The point isn't to use this specific micro-schedule but to develop a micro-schedule aligned to your district's program and curriculum.

The value of micro-schedules for the reading block strikes lots of people as common sense, so why aren't reading block micro-schedules more common? Based on many conversations with reading directors and principals, we think it's because staff either don't think a reading block micro-schedule is necessary or mistakenly believe they already have and follow one.

Staff who believe micro-schedules aren't needed usually say the curriculum is clear and tells teachers what to teach. This is typically only partially true. Yes, most

FIGURE 3.2

A Grade 1 Reading Block Micro-schedule

Activity	Time in Minutes
Whole-group read-aloud	15
Word study	10
Direct phonics instruction	20

Small-group work (rotation)
    Group 1: Decoding/fluency w/teacher
    Group 2: Individual/buddy reading
    Group 3: Vocabulary building
	45

Total	**90**

curricula do map out all the elements of effective reading instruction, but seldom does a curriculum provide the grade-by-grade, minutes-per-day level detail that a micro-schedule does. The other camp says, or maybe just hopes, that teachers already subdivide their reading blocks into a micro-schedule. The case of Moundsview should make it clear that leaving micro-scheduling up to teachers will likely result in lots of variation, and some plans will give short shrift to key aspects of the reading program. Despite the best of intentions and efforts, many teachers will stray from the desired plan. It may be unintended inequity, but it's inequity all the same.

Although these are the common explanations we encounter for the lack of micro-schedules for the reading block, perhaps there is a third reason that explains it best: issuing a micro-schedule is uncomfortable! The discomfort stems partially from school and district leaders not wanting to micromanage their people. "Teachers know their students best," the thinking goes. "It makes sense that the important teaching and learning decisions should be left up to them." And yes, teachers do know their students well, and they are professionals deserving of trust. But how many teachers are expert in the science of reading instruction? Many newer teachers we have worked with (and plenty of experienced ones too) are, in fact, very thankful to have more specific guidelines for their reading block because having them removes part of the guesswork from such an important part of a student's education.

The other source of discomfort is a reluctance to be specific. Many curriculum materials suggest a range of instructional times: 10–20 minutes for phonics, 20–40 minutes for small-group instruction, and so on. If you go with the top end of these recommended ranges (e.g., 20 minutes for phonics, 40 minutes for small-group instruction), it's common for the recommended instructional time to total 120 or even 140 minutes. We know it's hard to say, "Devote fewer minutes to phonics" or "Students need less time in small groups," but given that there are only 90 minutes to work with, someone must draw these lines. In our view, these decisions are best made by a small, thoughtful team that includes highly effective teachers—*not* by every teacher on their own. Making micro-schedule creation the responsibility of each individual teacher is stressful and time-consuming for staff, especially newer teachers, and too often, it's unfair to kids.

Staggering Grade-Level, Reading, Math, and Intervention (and Enrichment) Blocks

Obviously, the elementary master schedule gives direction to classroom teachers; it maps out how they should spend their time each day. A micro-schedule provides them with even more direction. But sometimes folks forget that the master schedule directly impacts many other staff in the school. It's the schedule for everyone, not just classroom teachers. In fact, the elementary master schedule also determines how effective special educators and reading teachers can be.

Here is a thought experiment: Imagine a classroom teacher driving to work alone. If they feel like stopping for coffee and have the time, it's no big deal if they do. Their preference guides the decision: *Do I want a coffee or not?* But what if several teachers were carpooling to work? Before stopping for coffee, the driver would need to check with everyone else in the car: "Does anyone mind? Do we all have time?" The front seat passenger has no objections ("Sure!"), but the back seat passenger does: "Well, I have a parent coming in this morning to talk with me before the first bell. With this traffic, I think it could be tight."

Too often, the master scheduler builds the schedule assuming every classroom teacher is "driving to work alone." With how interconnected the work of classroom teachers and other types of teachers are, one person's preference—or even a few people's preferences—can't be the only thing guiding the decision. We have met many a conscientious scheduler who keeps a list of teacher preferences on their desk or in their head as they build the schedule: those who want a morning reading block, those who prefer morning intervention, those who prefer end-of-day intervention, and so on. Yet the master schedule affects special educators, interventionists (like reading teachers), and English learner (EL) teachers as much as it does classroom teachers, and too often their needs aren't in the forefront when the master schedule is being built.

There are three teaching and learning best practices that are especially affected by both the master schedule and the schedules of special educators, EL teachers, and interventionists:

1. **No pullout during core reading and math.** Nearly all students, including students with mild to moderate disabilities, should receive 100 percent of core instruction in reading and math. They will never master current-year material if they aren't in the room while it's being taught. The extra help and services they receive should be extra—in addition to, not instead of, core instruction.

2. **Intervention grouped by area of need.** A reading intervention block, for example, will be more impactful if everyone in the group has the same focus area, be it phonics or fluency or something else.

3. **Intervention provided by content-strong teachers.** Who provides students with extra help matters a lot. Highly skilled teachers with subject specific training, interest, and aptitude are most effective.

Imagine a special educator or reading teacher who wants to embrace these three best practices but can't because the master schedule wasn't designed with this goal in mind. For example, if all the teachers in the school teach reading in the morning, then speech therapists and other related service providers have no choice but to pull some students out of the reading block to receive services. They can't simply *not* provide services all morning long; it would be impossible to squeeze all their work into the afternoon hours. A master schedule that staggers reading and math blocks throughout the day is a way to ensure that the related service providers can serve some students in the morning and some in the afternoon, protecting every student's core instruction time.

Turns out that it is best to stagger intervention blocks. If the whole school has intervention at the same time, certified intervention staff are in the untenable situation of providing extra help to hundreds of students at the same time. In most schools, when there aren't enough certified teachers to provide reading support, students with special needs tend to get reading help from paraprofessionals, while their non-disabled peers get instruction from certified staff. Perversely, the students with the greatest need get instructors with less training. Not only is this not a best practice, but it's also a long-standing cause of inequity. It's wrong and unfair, and strategic schedules can address the issue.

So, while it's unwise to synchronize all reading and math blocks or all intervention schoolwide, what schedulers *can* synchronize to positive effect is *grade-level* intervention: intervention blocks that are staggered by grade but common within grades—the kindergarten intervention block at 9:00 a.m., the 1st grade intervention block at 10:00 a.m., and so on. Within this scenario, perhaps 100 1st graders might need extra help or enrichment. The school could "flood the grade" with, say, seven certified teachers (a combination of the 1st grade classroom teachers and special educators, reading teachers, and ELL teachers). Each of these teachers would deliver targeted instruction to a subset of students drawn from different 1st grade classrooms. The reading teacher, for example, might head up a best-practice intervention group of 1st graders who are all struggling with vowel sounds. For even more smaller groups, a few paraprofessionals might be brought into lead groups that will receive enrichment (but not intervention, please).

None of these teaching and learning best practices would be possible if the master schedule weren't designed with the mental model that teachers are carpooling to work, not driving alone. Figure 3.3 shows a snapshot of one such schedule that staggers intervention and core reading and math while maintaining consistency at each grade level.

Providing Common Grade-Level Planning Time

Having specials, math, reading, and other time blocks similar by grade level but staggered across the school day provides a bonus benefit: automatic common planning time for grade-level teachers. When it's done well, teachers planning together can help improve teaching and learning.

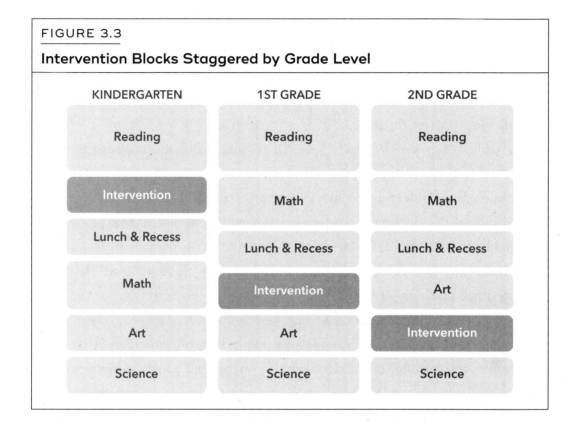

FIGURE 3.3

Intervention Blocks Staggered by Grade Level

KINDERGARTEN	1ST GRADE	2ND GRADE
Reading	Reading	Reading
Intervention	Math	Math
Lunch & Recess	Lunch & Recess	Lunch & Recess
Math	Intervention	Art
Art	Art	Intervention
Science	Science	Science

When Specials Get in the Way

Very often, a principal who sits down to build a strategic schedule with clear priorities; time blocks that fit into the school day; and a willingness to stagger reading, math, and common grade-level intervention time throughout the day will hit a wall when it comes to specials: art, music, PE, and so on. More precisely, the wall they hit is specials *staffing*.

This is less a scheduling problem than a cart-and-horse problem. When a cart gets in front of the horse meant to pull it, the cart can't move, even though there isn't anything wrong with the cart. The problem is taking the current special staffing and rotation of specials offerings as fixed and immutable—something to schedule *around*, similar to how the cafeteria capacity dictates lunch schedules. Though it's very hard to make a cafeteria larger, tweaking specials staffing isn't nearly as difficult, especially if the central office is part of the scheduling team.

One large district spent two years preparing to implement strategic elementary schedules. They created thoughtful time blocks, clear non-negotiables, and a good reading micro-schedule. They committed to all seven of the best practices on our list. But then 18 of the district's 22 elementary schools abandoned ship because they couldn't fit in all the required specials with the staff they had. As part of the budgeting process conducted months earlier, the central office had set the specials staffing levels such that schools would share art, music, and PE staff. It identified which days and what time of day art, music and PE teachers would be in each school. Given these constraints, there was little the principals could do to build the schedules they wanted and kids deserved.

What saved the strategic scheduling effort in this district was a *willingness* to adjust specials scheduling and staffing—to see them as an accelerator of strategic scheduling rather than an obstacle. The elementary principals listed when they needed specialists in their building. A central office coordinator helped make sense of all the requests and helped adjust the rotation of specials in a few schools; a month later, all 22 schools had strategic schedules. In the end, the district needed to bring in only 0.4 FTE of additional staff across nearly two dozen elementary schools. Yes, changes were made to specialists' building assignments and schedules, but this gave more than 13,000 students schedules that allowed them access to best practices in teaching and learning.

◆ ◆ ◆

The elementary master schedule has a lot of influence for something that generally fits on a single sheet of copy paper. The master schedule directs how and where teachers spend their day, how much time goes to each subject, whether SEL and intervention really happen, and whether all members of a school staff can embrace the best practices that drive student learning.

The toughest part of being a great elementary master scheduler is being willing to make hard choices when setting priorities—things like combining reading and social studies or trimming science to make time for intervention. You need to hold firm on what's crucial and be flexible on what's not. **The next step toward developing an elementary master schedule is to complete the self-assessment in Appendix A** (see p. 200). It will help you take stock of your current schedule and identify how well it aligns with all the best practices we have highlighted.

4

Creating the (Many) Other Elementary Schedules

*Strategically schedule intervention,
special education, and related services*

Here is a seemingly simple question: *How many schedules does one elementary school need?* Hint: it's more than one.

Too often, school and district leaders put 99 percent of their energy and thought into building a single elementary schedule per school: the master schedule. Though the master schedule is definitely important, it's not the only important schedule in an elementary school. To supercharge learning, especially in an era of large achievement gaps and widespread learning loss, school and district leaders also need to actively plan and manage the schedules of reading teachers, special educators, related service providers, English language (EL) teachers, and other interventionists.

In most schools, these important "other" schedules are built by the teacher themselves, typically with little help and even less oversight. You might be wondering, "What's the problem? Smart, caring teachers are building their own schedules, and it seems to work just fine. Why not leave things as is?" The short answer is because teachers building their own schedule is *not* really working fine.

Why *All* Staff Need Strategic Schedules

Asking every reading teacher, special educator, EL teacher, and other interventionist to build their own schedule isn't best for kids, the budget, or the teachers themselves. To be clear, this is not a knock on these staff members. They are caring, hardworking, smart folks doing the best anyone can within a system that doesn't place enough importance on their schedules.

Making all the schedules in an elementary school strategic schedules will allow you to do the following:

- Expand the reach of intervention and special education teachers so that they can help (a lot) more students without being overloaded.
- Improve teacher work-life balance and reduce staff stress.
- Make intervention more impactful.
- Make core instruction more successful.

Perhaps the most important reason to want strategic schedules for all these other types of teachers in an elementary school is because these teachers are so important. Reading teachers can change lives, special educators make an enormous difference for kids with disabilities, and EL teachers can open new worlds. They and their time are important, and so, by extension, are their schedules.

The Complexity of the Challenge

The importance and complexity of scheduling these positions hit home for Nate when the district he led found itself short of both reading teachers and special educators. About a month into the school year, it had become clear that the district was understaffed in certified reading teachers and couldn't fill a few special education vacancies. The principals and special education director got together to figure out what they could do. The plan that emerged included tightening the criteria for who would receive reading intervention and informing the parents of students with disabilities that compensatory services would be provided later in the year. Essentially, they had made a plan to do less.

Having already committed to robust reading intervention for all who needed it, and having promised the special education parents association that the district would eliminate missed services, this plan felt more like managing failure than finding a winning strategy. So Nate pushed back. How could they help all the kids who needed help with the staff they had?

The principals and special education director pushed back harder. "We can't overload the teachers we have," one principal said. "They will leave, and then we will be in even worse shape."

"If our current staff could cover all the kids who need help, we wouldn't have asked for the extra FTE," reminded the special education director.

"You can't get blood from a stone," another principal said, and this statement was met with much head nodding from the other principals in the room.

It was clear to Nate that a solution would not emerge from that meeting, so he scheduled another—this one with all the reading teachers and elementary special educators. Nate laid out the problem: the district was short-staffed, and the students would suffer. "What could we do to serve all the kids without overloading you?" Nate asked. "Is there a win-win?"

These questions were met with silence. A few folks muttered they were already working nights and weekends and couldn't believe Nate was asking for more. One reading teacher said, "A win-win solution? Definitely not possible—not with the schedule I have."

Her phrasing struck Nate as odd, so he asked her to say more. She went on to explain that she was already teaching seven groups a day and couldn't fit in even one more group. "I mean, if I could pull one more student into each of my seven groups, I could help seven more students," she mused, "but that's impossible."

"Why impossible?" Nate asked.

The reading teacher explained that the classroom teachers would not let her have the students at times when she could take them because it would pull them out of important core instruction.

At that point, a special educator jumped in with a comment: "I *wish* I could have seven groups in a day! I'm lucky if I have time for four groups. Mostly, I just pull out the kids when I need them. No one says no to me, because compliance demands I take the students when I'm available."

For Nate, this meeting was more troubling than the one he'd had with the administrators. Here is what he learned:

- The district's reading teachers had seven group sessions a day, with each session lasting 30 minutes. This amounted to just three and a half hours of teaching per day. He knew elementary classroom teachers provided direct instruction for five and half hours per day.

- These reading teachers had to negotiate with classroom teachers to get access to students.

- The district's special educators provided direct instruction for less than two and half hours each day, but legal compliance with the IDEA meant they had much easier access to students.

- Nearly all the teachers present struggled to build their schedules; it often took a few weeks of back-and-forth with classroom teachers before everything was set. Some felt they could persuade the classroom teacher to be "flexible," and others didn't even try. No one helped them build their schedules or resolve conflicts with classroom teachers.

Puzzled by the discussion, Nate asked everyone present to share with him their schedule and student groupings from the previous week. When we analyzed their schedules, some additional data points emerged:

- Some reading teachers taught 20 students per week, others 30, and one 40.

- Some special educators had four groups a day, others five, and a few had six.

- On average, reading groups were 50 percent larger than special education groups, even though both kinds of groups were receiving similar academic support.

Given the importance of reading and special education services, it was surprising that so much was left to chance, to the individual teacher, or to past practice. Over the next 30 days, a scheduling guru (a teacher in the district) revamped all these schedules, treating them as strategically important. At the end of the month, Nate's district had solved their "staffing crises"—not by adding FTEs but by doing the following:

1. Establishing common language and work expectations that allowed them to extend the reach of existing staff without overloading them.
2. Having principals coordinate with classroom teachers to release more students for reading, special education, and English language learning and adding these students to existing intervention groups.
3. Creating a fixed time each week for IEP meetings and clarifying when reading and special education teachers' attendance was required.

Read on to learn more about why these measures are effective and how working as a team of staff and administrators can transform your existing intervention and special education schedules into strategic schedules.

Increasing Reach

The most startling insight Nate got from that meeting with reading and special education teachers was there wasn't an agreed-upon definition of, or expectation for, what constituted a "full schedule"—not for them or for related services and EL staff. Equally startling was that no principal or central office leader had a definition of a full schedule either. Having since surveyed more than 200 districts, Nate can report that this omission is sadly common: very few districts have set clear expectations for a full teaching load for reading teachers, special education staff, or other staff in similar roles. If reading teachers in School A teach five groups a day and reading teachers in School B teach seven, then one school will help 10 fewer students. What's more, the principal of School A will feel understaffed, lamenting that some kids who need reading help just can't get it. The lack of expectations for what is a reasonable group size can also lead to some schools underserving kids in need.

This lack of guidelines stands in total contrast to how general education teachers are treated. All districts set very specific parameters for class size, the amount of time a classroom teacher will be in the room, and the number of sections elementary specialists and secondary teachers will teach. For these folks, what constitutes a full schedule is explicitly set by school and district leaders: five periods a day for high school teachers, 24 periods a week for elementary art teachers, and so on. To be fair, most principals were never special educators, which could explain a reluctance to set some workload expectations, and central office leaders tend not to want to "micromanage" school-based staff.

Strategic schedules address not just how many groups are scheduled for reading, special education, and other interventional services each day for each FTE but also how many kids, on average, are in each group. They provide expectations for these staff members to maximize their reach and, thus, increase their impact.

Reach is the number of students served by one FTE. It can be calculated with a simple formula:

Reach = [Number of groups taught per day] × [Average group size]

If a reading teacher, say, teaches five groups, and each group contains four students, that teacher's reach is 20 students. If that same teacher teaches eight groups, and each group has five students, the teacher's reach is 40 students. That's twice the number of kids helped. The matrix in Figure 4.1 depicts this difference and illustrates various other reach scenarios possible for a single intervention teacher teaching multiple small-group sessions throughout the day.

Different districts can reasonably set different expectations for what they think is a reasonable reach for all types of staff. Not setting any expectation, however, is a missed opportunity. Let's now examine both parts of the reach equation in more detail to see how you can maximize the impact of highly valued staff at your school.

How many hours each day should be spent with students?

Strategic schedules begin with setting an expectation for how many groups an interventionist, special educator, EL teacher, and so on should lead each day. It's a good place to start because the number of groups a teacher or related service provider works with in a given day is determines how much time they spend directly working with students.

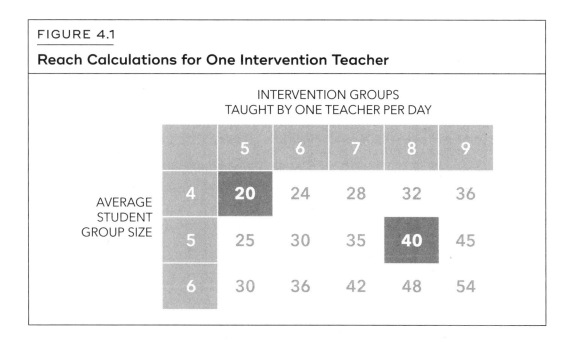

FIGURE 4.1

Reach Calculations for One Intervention Teacher

The number of groups taught typically differs by role. A reading teacher might teach nine groups per day, for example, while a special educator (who has many other responsibilities) might teach just six. One district team in New Jersey sat down to figure out a fair teaching schedule for their reading teachers, who were highly skilled. The team started by getting some baseline data: How many groups did each reading teacher currently teach every day? Most taught five, one taught six, and one taught seven. The first reaction was that five seemed reasonable—in line with the number of classes that the district's high school teachers taught in a day. The superintendent and head of reading thought this logic was sound, but it gave Nate pause. He pointed out a few things:

- Because each group met for 30 minutes, each highly skilled, much-in-demand reading teacher would work with kids for a total of just two and a half hours per day. This didn't seem to maximize the benefit of some of the most talented folks in the district.
- Elementary classroom teachers taught nearly six hours of every seven-hour school day, with 40 minutes reserved for planning and preparation and 30 minutes for lunch.

- High school teachers did teach five periods each day, but because each high school period was 55 minutes long, they were teaching for a total of four and a half hours a day.

With this context added, five groups and two and a half hours a day of teaching reading seemed wrong—with an underutilization of staff and an unnecessary limit on their reach. The group quickly concluded that eight groups (four hours of teaching a day) would be the new minimum. Ultimately, the team agreed that parity with other staff meant nine groups would be the full teaching load for reading teachers.

The process was repeated for special educators, but it was necessarily more nuanced. First, because special education staff provide various kinds of support, the district's team reframed the question, changing "How many groups should each teacher teach?" to "How much of the school day should special education staff devote to providing direct services to students?" They also considered that various roles under the umbrella term "special education staff," reasoning that the differences in the work responsibilities of elementary special education teachers, secondary special education teachers, teachers in substantially separate classrooms, related service providers, and school psychologists justified generating a unique set of time-with-students expectations for each staff role.

It might seem like common sense that a discussion of a reasonable teaching load would start by looking at current teaching loads. But doing this can lock in some less-than-optimal past practices. By coincidence, we were helping two school districts build strategic schedules for special educators at the same time. The two districts were nearly identical in size, demographics, and per-pupil spending. They were each large and low spending, but that's where the similarities ended.

In one of the districts (let's call it District A), special educators spent about 30 percent of the day working with kids. The rest of the day was devoted to meetings, assessing for IEPs, and writing very lengthy IEPs. District leadership wanted to increase special educators' direct service time to 50 percent and defined *direct service percentage* as hours per week providing instruction to students divided by the contractual work week. Staff howled. "This is humanly impossible," said many. A few added it was just cruel and would force teachers to leave.

In District B, on the other hand, special educators spent 65 percent of their day with students, and leadership was committed to getting this to 75 percent. Working with teams of special educators, District B mapped out ways to streamline meetings and speed up the paperwork, strip away some clerical tasks, and brainstorm other ways to free up time during the day. The staff viewed the exercise as exciting. They wanted to spend more time with kids—that's why they became teachers in the first place.

Three years later, special educators in District B had reached their goal of spending 75 percent of the day working with students, but District A was struggling to reach 33 percent. The difference can be explained by both expectations and systems thinking. You can't just wish for more time with students. The gains in District B were only possible after a deep dive into how time was used and proactive steps to streamline meetings and paperwork while still ensuring near 100 percent compliance. For more on how to free up the time of special educators and improve their work life, see Nate's book *Six Shifts to Improve Special Education and Other Interventions* (Levenson, 2020).

Based on work with more than 250 districts and a review of more than 50,000 staff schedules, we have created some benchmarks for what's typical and what's possible in terms of staff time with students. Figure 4.2 shares a few gold standards for some of the most common roles.

What about the teachers, though? If you are thinking, "OK, increasing reach could be helpful to kids, but this will stress out already-stressed staff," don't fret. Two steps can allow for increased reach *and* increased job satisfaction. The first, detailed in Nate's book, is streamlining meetings and paperwork (see Levenson, 2020). The second is to form groups of students who have similar needs. We'll look more closely at homogeneous grouping practices in a moment, but first, a few words about streamlining. Simply put, it's unfair to add more sessions to a teacher's day without first taking something away. Too often the time staff spend *not* working with kids is considered unalterable, so the direct service time is limited to what's left over. Strategic schedules flip this thinking upside down.

FIGURE 4.2

Time-with-Students Benchmarks

Role	% of Day Providing Direct Instruction/ Services to Students	
	Typical	Gold Standard
Special education teacher: working with students with mild to moderate disabilities	30–45%	65%
Special education teacher: working with students with severe disabilities	80%	80%
Reading teacher	45–50%	75%
EL teacher	40–50%	65%
Speech and language therapist	30–45%	65%
Social worker	30–35%	75%

One district came to realize that their reading teachers spent only 40 percent of the day with kids and their counselors just 30 percent. Though everyone wanted to see direct service rise to 65 percent, it just didn't seem realistic. The district asked the staff what they would have to stop doing or do differently to have 65 percent of their day available to work with kids. After a few days to ponder this question, here is what they shared:

- "I would have to stop going to every IEP meeting and just attend the ones where reading was an issue."
- "I would not attend every discipline meeting, just the ones where I had been working with the student already."
- "A paraprofessional would have to run the reading score reports, print them, and share with the PLCs each week."

On they went, and within an hour, they had identified many reasonable things to stop doing. It wasn't that these activities weren't of value; they just weren't nearly as valuable as working with students. By fixing 65 percent of direct service, it was possible to adjust indirect service to fit the time alloted.

Reach Factor 2: How many students should be in a group?

The second half of the reach question concerns the number of students that are in a typical group. For special educators, reading teachers, and the like, group size is equivalent to class size for a classroom teacher, and the comparison to general education is stark. If you ask any principal about the average class size in their school, they will know it to a decimal place. Ask how it varies by grade, and most will be able tell you off the top of their head. Now ask the same principal or district leader how many students are in the typical reading group or special education resource room. Few will be able to answer. Give them a week to research, and most will come back surprised that the answer does not live in any database or student information system.

When leaders do finally calculate the average group size, they are surprised how small it usually is. In most schools there is an opportunity to increase the reach of reading teachers, special educators, and EL staff by slightly increasing the size of groups. But won't increasing group size overload teachers and water down instruction? Not if the groups are formed to include only students with similar areas of need—the homogenous grouping approach we mentioned earlier. Turns out that teaching a group of five students with near-identical needs can be easier and more effective than teaching a group of three students with very different needs.

Let's look at two reading groups. Group A has three students and Group B has five. If this is all the information available, Group A certainly seems better for kids and easier to teach. We have to dig deeper, though. Group A is small, but it was formed based on student availability, typically being in the same general education classroom. One student struggles with phonics, another has difficulty with comprehension, and the third needs help with fluency. With three different areas of need, Group A is actually complicated to teach; each student gets only about 10 minutes of help per session that is targeted to their top need. Group B's five students, in contrast, all struggle with the same thing (phonics), so everybody's chief need is addressed throughout the entire session. Some schools take this a step further by creating hyper-focused groups of students who all struggle with, say, the long vowel sounds in phonics.

So: strategic schedules don't prioritize small group sizes; they prioritize reach, effectiveness, and teacher work life, which means setting reasonable group sizes and grouping by area of need.

Many are surprised to hear that in intervention settings, smaller groups aren't always better groups. Research backs this up. The instructor's training and background, the length of intervention time provided, and the type of instruction presented during intervention are all more significant factors for increasing student achievement than intervention group size (Vaughn et al., 2012).

Studies by the What Works Clearinghouse have shown that small instructional groups of up to five students are as effective as one-on-one instruction (Gersten et al., 2008). Similarly, the National Institute of Health has shown that intervention groups of three students can be as effective as one-on-one instruction, and that even groups of up to 10 students can provide benefits, although with smaller outcomes on achievement (Vaughn et al., 2010). (Notably, this study did not test or include groups of four to nine students.) More specifically, the RTI Action Network recommends intervention groups of five to eight students for the majority of students who struggle and smaller groups of one to three for students with severe reading disabilities (Harlacher et al., 2014).

This research confirms that proactively managing intervention group size becomes a mechanism by which a district can expand the reach of its highly skilled teachers of reading and others.

The Perils of Poorly Scheduled Pullout

Students can't be in two places at the same time, so it's important to remember that every time a student is added to an interventionist's or special educator's schedule, they are missing something else. After reviewing nearly 50,000 staff schedules, it's clear to us that many schools prioritize making sure every student who needs help receives that extra help; what they miss when they are pulled out of class to receive it is of secondary importance. A desire to help and a fear of noncompliance seem to explain this reality.

Unfortunately, pullout can unintentionally harm the very students staff are trying to help. Best practices call for providing extra help that is *extra,* not *instead of.* This means that students should never be pulled from core reading and math instruction. All the other important supports provided to them *are* important, but they should be scheduled during the other four hours of the school day—the hours not devoted to core instruction in reading and math. Recently, many of the districts we work with have passed policies or set "non-negotiables" to ensure that nearly 100 percent of students get 100 percent of core reading and math time. Yes, a small number of kids have highly specialized needs; they are the exception to this rule.

Too often principals and teachers say, "This is a great idea in theory, but it just doesn't work in the real world." Over the last decade, we have helped build more than 500 elementary school schedules, and every school was able to create special education and intervention schedules that did not conflict with reading and math instruction. A more accurate comment would be "You know, this is a great idea, and we will have to make some changes to our schedules and to how we create our schedules to make it work in the real world."

There are three steps to providing extra-time support to students without pulling them out of core reading and math instruction.

1. **Don't accept anything less than 100 percent core instruction.** This arrangement is not just nice to have; it's a must-have. No other priority should be higher on an elementary school's list. If a principal or teacher can't figure out how to ensure 100 percent of students get 100 percent of core reading and math, get someone else to help create the schedule.

2. **Stagger the reading and math blocks.** In some schools, all the classes teach reading right after morning meeting, and many teach math just before lunch. If everyone teaches math and reading at the same time, then special educators or reading teachers or speech therapists don't have any choice but to pull

some kids during these shouldn't-miss periods. They can't have hours each day when all their students are unavailable.

3. **Organize scheduling parties.** If everyone builds their schedule alone, then whoever schedules last often can't find a time that works for their caseload and honors the never-pull-from-core-reading-and-math rule. Scheduling parties can fix this. A scheduling party is when the principal and the reading teachers, the special educators, the EL teachers, and related service folks all get in a room and build their schedules at the same time. If someone can't find a spot for a required service that honors the no-pullout rule, then they can work with their colleagues and move things around in real time. Ideally, a scheduling expert will also be in the room to help. If the principal brings a few pizzas or pastries, it's a small party too.

One large district we worked with that had lots of staff shared between schools and found it often pulled students at inopportune times took the scheduling party concept to scale. They had 70 school principals come to a large gymnasium and sit at 70 tables. All the special education staff came to the gym to build their schedules, sitting at the principal's table with the other folks who serviced students in that school. When scheduling conflicts or a bottleneck arose, everyone who needed to "flex their schedule" was already in the room. The district's central office also provided a few scheduling experts to help as needed. The first year, the process took two and a half days. The following year, all the schedules got built in less than one day. Going forward, no student in that district was ever again pulled from reading and math to receive extra help or special education services.

A Caution About "Push-In" Models

It's true that strategic schedules make it possible to ensure that all students receive 100 percent of core reading and math without adding staff or lengthening the school day. That said, some schools struggle to build strategic schedules because they didn't follow the three suggestions above or they haven't yet developed the skills of a great scheduler. Remember, hardly anyone learns how to build schedules when training to become a teacher or principal.

When it seems just darn impossible to honor the no-pullout rule, some schools opt for a "clever" alternative. They adopt a push-in model, where the speech therapist, special educator, reading teacher, or other support provider goes into the general education classroom during core reading or math instruction. *A perfect solution,* they think. *Kids don't miss a minute of key subjects, and with two teachers in the room, they can supercharge learning as well.* Unfortunately, this isn't actually a solution that will work for most students.

In this model, kids who struggle lose out on extra-time intervention. For example, rather than getting 90 minutes of core reading plus 30 minutes of intervention for a total of 120 minutes of daily reading instruction, they get just 90 minutes of reading. This is the same amount of instruction provided to the kids who *don't* struggle with reading. For the kids who struggle, 90 minutes isn't enough. They need dedicated time for re-teaching, pre-teaching, and learning skills from the prior year that they haven't yet mastered. Worse yet, based on many hundreds of observations, we have concluded that the push-in model doesn't solve the problem it was designed to: protecting student's core instruction time. True, kids are in the room for 100 percent of the core lesson—but if the second adult talks to them, works with them, teaches a mini-lesson, or does almost anything, then the students' attention is pulled away from the core lesson. Kids can't listen to two adults at the same time.

◆ ◆ ◆

Every elementary school has a lot more schedules beyond the master schedule, and all these schedules are interconnected. Strategic scheduling is as much a mindset as it is a set of technical skills. It asks folks to build every schedule with all the other schedules in mind. If everyone builds a great schedule alone, the final set of schedules won't collectively be great.

Strategic schedulers remember that special educators, reading teachers, EL staff, and other interventionists are all carpooling to school, not driving there alone. They also never forget that interventionists are highly skilled and that their time is precious; every minute of their day is treated as such.

The next two chapters will outline how scheduling best practices must be handled a bit differently at the middle school and the ways in which schedules in grades 6 through 8 should reflect the changing needs of students as they transition into adolescence.

Middle School

5

Making Middle School Schedules More Strategic

Blend the middle school model with scheduling best practices

Middle school years are a complicated time. Students are grown up compared to their elementary school peers but a lot less mature than high schoolers. As the name implies, they are in the middle—a spot between being young children and independent adults. Back in the 1970s and 1980s, the middle school movement took hold to better address the unique social-emotional and academic needs of 6th, 7th, and 8th graders. According to the National Center for Education Statistics, the number of middle schools in the country rose 462 percent from 1970 to 2000, while the number of junior high schools declined by 57 percent (Snyder & Dillow, 2011). By the 2000s, nearly every district in the United States had embraced some form of the middle school model.

The traditional middle school approach often includes grade-level teaching teams, grade-level planning time, a focus on student emotional well-being (long before SEL became a priority at other grade levels), and a schedule that tends to be built grade by grade. Many middle schools have three master schedules: a 6th grade schedule, a 7th grade one, and an 8th grade version. The grade-level schedules try to keep teachers to a single grade and seldom mix students across grades. Some aspects of the traditional middle school schedule are very beneficial. Experts assert that teaming is uniquely advantageous for middle school students because it promotes student bonding and fosters closer relationships between teachers and students. Additionally, teaming promotes interdisciplinary instruction and coordination, especially when teacher teams receive common planning time (Hanover Research, 2016).

The middle school model also seems to enjoy great support from middle school teachers and middle school administrators. Actually, that's an understatement; many school-based staff seem to *love* their middle school model. It's common for attempts to change middle school schedules to lead to fierce debate, fueled by a fear that what's great about middle schools will disappear in the new schedule. After consulting in more than 250 districts in 30 states, we have seen how attempts to revise middle school schedules often lead to low staff morale, ill will, contentious board meetings, and more than a few superintendents losing their jobs. We have watched thoughtful, politically adept district leaders engage middle school staff in a multi-year, inclusive schedule redesign process only to abandon ship before implementing many worthwhile changes to the schedule.

Why New Middle School Schedules Are Necessary

After reading the last paragraph, you might be thinking that we recommend against revising middle school schedules—but think again. Though it's not easy, it's worth the effort. Even though middle school staff more often than not *like* the schedule they have, there is a growing body of evidence to suggest that middle school students, staff, and budgets would all benefit from strategic middle school schedules. And there's a growing number of district leaders who support this move.

Many students dip academically in middle school grades; this is the case even in K–8 schools, which have had better outcomes, on average, than traditional grade 6–8 middle schools. The academic loss helps to explain why far too many 9th graders are ill-prepared to succeed academically in high school (West & Schwerdt, 2012). The dip is particularly problematic because struggling in 9th grade is a strong indicator of dropping out of school in later grades.

In the post–COVID pandemic world, many middle school teachers are stressed by the challenge of helping students master grade-level requirements even though they have gaps from interrupted prior learning and are less engaged. As you will learn, strategic middle school schedules supercharge intervention and student engagement, which helps bring back more of the joy of being a middle school teacher.

It's also important to point out that classic middle schools cost 20–25 percent more per student to teach than a strategic middle school schedule, based on our analysis of middle schools across the country. Though many middle schools serve their students well, and not every challenge in high school is linked to the middle school schedule, a strategic middle school schedule can boost learning while respecting that middle schools and middle schoolers are different from elementary and high school students. In short, a strategic middle school schedule honors the middle school model while further improving outcomes.

A *strategic* middle school schedule differs from many classic middle school schedules in a few important ways. Strategic middle school schedules

1. Provide sufficient time for core instruction.
2. Provide best-practice intervention for students who struggle academically.
3. Define equity as every student getting what they need.
4. Maximize the impact of teacher planning time.
5. Engage students in their passions while giving them the opportunity to discover new ones.
6. Create meaningful bonds between students and staff.
7. Do all the above in a cost-effective way.

This chapter addresses the first four points and shares some lessons learned about how to work with teachers and school leaders to collaboratively develop strategic middle school schedules. Chapter 6 focuses on points 5 and 6 (student passions and relationship building—major components of the middle school model), and Chapter 10 addresses the impact strategic scheduling at all levels has on the budget.

Providing Sufficient Time for Core Instruction

As students mature from elementary school to middle school, they change in many ways—evolving physically and emotionally and solidifying their sense of self. One thing that doesn't change, however, is the importance of learning math, English language arts (ELA), science, and social studies. Yes, this might seem like an obvious point, but after reviewing many hundreds of middle school schedules, we know it's a point that still must be made.

Based on nearly 20 years of analyzing middle school schedules from across the country, we have seen that most provide 6th, 7th, and 8th graders less time to master math, English, and other core subjects than their elementary and high school peers. Analyzing time dedicated to math instruction is an enlightening case in point.

Our research and work with schools has taught us that typical 5th grader in a U.S. elementary school has 60 minutes of math each day, and the typical high school student has a single 52- to 55-minute math period each day. The typical U.S. middle school students get 45 minutes of math per day. Maybe you are thinking, "It's just a few minutes less per day—who cares? Why all the anxiety over a few minutes?" We care because those few minutes add up, as depicted in Figure 5.1. When math instruction is delivered in 45-minute periods each day, middle school students receive 135 hours of math instruction a year, which is 25 percent less than elementary students (180 hours per year) and 13 percent less than high school students (156 hours per year).

Remember, one key research finding discussed in Chapter 2 is the strong correlation between learning and the amount of quality instructional time (Aronson et al., 1998). More time spent teaching a subject generally translates into more learning in that subject, provided that both instruction and curriculum are of high quality. When folks first designed middle school schedules, we don't think they assumed that there was less math to teach and learn in grades 6 through 8, or that the content was so much simpler that it could be taught and learned that much quicker. Our sense is that the schedule designers had other priorities in mind, and the shorter core periods were more of an outcome of other decisions than an intentional design element.

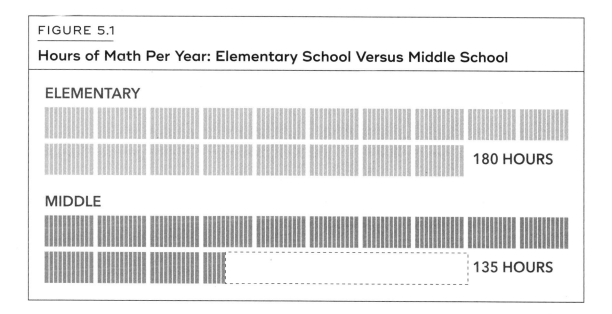

FIGURE 5.1

Hours of Math Per Year: Elementary School Versus Middle School

ELEMENTARY

180 HOURS

MIDDLE

135 HOURS

Here's an example to highlight the drawback of core subject blocks' length being more of an afterthought than a plan. Some large districts have a wide range of grade configurations: K–5 schools, K–6 schools, K–8 schools, grades 6–8 schools, and so on. Imagine two students in this district, Nate and David. Nate attends a K–5 school, then a grades 6–8 middle school. As a 6th grader, he receives 135 hours of math instruction. David lives in another part of town and attends a K–6 school, then a grade 7–8 junior high. In his 6th grade year, he receives 180 hours of math instruction. Though the district's school grade configurations are different, the textbook students use, the curriculum they're taught, and the state test they take are the same. When you compare 135 hours of instruction to 180 hours of instruction, it's hard to see how David isn't at a disadvantage for learning math. This seems to be a source of inequity, and if David wants a career in a STEM field, it might be a life-altering arrangement.

A well-rounded, engaging education includes more than just core subjects, but the modern world of high standards does require mastery of much content and many skills. A strategic middle school schedule provides ample time for core subject classes—typically no less than 50 minutes a day.

Providing Best-Practice Intervention

If all students receive a reasonable dose of core instruction, some will still need extra time to master important content. A 50-plus-minute period per subject should be enough time for a student who started the year on grade level and learns at a typical pace. Unfortunately, there will always be students starting the school year with skill gaps. This was true before the COVID-19 pandemic, and two years of disrupted learning have only increased the number of students who are struggling academically. Strategic middle school schedules ensure that students who need extra help get the help they need. This is a commitment to equity as well as to excellence.

As discussed in Chapter 2, best-practice research provides a clear and compelling roadmap for catching kids up academically. Students who struggle academically need effective core instruction plus extra time to learn from a content-strong teacher (Grossman, 2021). The extra time is used to teach foundational skills, address content not yet mastered from prior years, re-teach current content in new ways, and pre-teach important upcoming lessons. There is a lot to cover, and one extra period a day is just barely enough to get it all in.

Effective intervention takes time, and it also needs a skilled teacher to lead it. The most impactful intervention comes from direct instruction delivered by a teacher who knows the material inside and out. Simply sitting a student in front of a Chromebook to move through a software-based intervention program seldom gets the job done. Absent an invested adult to motivate them and an experienced teacher to help them navigate roadblocks, students who struggle learn little more than how to trick a computer program into reporting that they are actively engaged.

So, intervention teachers must teach. They must teach the skills and concepts that each student in the room hasn't yet mastered. To make the task even more complicated, interventionists need more than one way to teach each concept. Given that every student in an intervention class has already been exposed to the material without mastering it, presenting the material the exact same way a second time isn't likely to be any more successful than the first time. Varying instructional approaches until students "get it" requires teachers who have a deep understanding of the subject. Additionally, intervention teachers with subject matter expertise can see a wrong answer, deduce where the student went wrong in process or understanding, and then target instruction to "unteach" the incorrect approach or premise.

The final aspect of effective intervention is that it should be deep, not wide. By this, we mean schools that have dramatically closed the achievement gap allow students to concentrate on catching up in just one subject for at least half a year. Rather than trying to address multiple subjects at once, such as spreading intervention time across English, math, and science (for example), it's better to provide intensive extra help in just one subject. This allows enough time to achieve meaningful growth, which greatly increases student motivation.

These best practices are similar to what's shared in the elementary and high school chapters, because the same best practices apply. Yes, these practices look a little different at each level, but the big ideas are the same. Despite this similarity in need and solution, most middle schools schedules we have studied take a very different approach to intervention than their elementary and high school counterparts. The biggest difference is that few middle schools provide best-practice intervention, and many provide little to no intervention at all for students without documented disabilities. This lack of middle school intervention seems problematic given the 2019 Nation's Report Card finding that 66 percent of all U.S. 8th graders were not proficient in math and (coincidentally) 66 percent of U.S. 8th graders were not proficient in English language arts (National Assessment of Educational Progress, 2019a, 2019b). And again, this was before the pandemic!

Intervention efforts that fall short

To be fair, many middle schools work hard to support students who struggle and invest time, talent, and energy into the effort, but some common approaches to middle school intervention are in direct conflict with the best practices. Let's review the most common middle school strategies for helping students who struggle and see how they stack up.

The double block. Some middle schools provide two periods of a subject to all students. The most common flavor of this is all 6th graders having two periods of

ELA each day. This certainly provides extra time to catch up, and the instruction is from a content-strong teacher (both best practices), but it falls short in other ways. In these schools there is usually no extra-time intervention in 7th or 8th grade and none in math at any grade. It can also be unproductive for students who *aren't* struggling in ELA to take it twice every day.

Co-teaching. It's not surprising that schools that have embraced teams of general education teachers working together as part the middle school model also embrace co-teaching for students with disabilities. Co-teaching is the practice of having two teachers, a general education teacher and a special education teacher, teach together in the general ed classroom. During math, for example, the two teachers work together during the core math class. Though students with disabilities may have a requirement in their IEP for two teachers, all the students in the class can benefit, so the thinking goes.

Many schools and teachers really like co-teaching. Unfortunately, John Hattie's comprehensive study of co-teaching, included in *Visible Learning* (2008), reveals that co-teaching, on average, is not effective and may even reduce student learning. There are many reasons for this lackluster finding, and they are are discussed in detail in Nate's book *Six Shifts to Improve Special Education and Other Interventions* (Levenson, 2020). The most prevalent shortcomings of co-teaching are that it doesn't provide extra time to learn or teach prior content and skills, and that too often, the special education teacher in the co-teaching arrangement is tasked with answering questions from students with special needs despite lacking subject matter expertise.

The flex block or "all hands on deck." A strategy that seems to be gaining popularity, especially in the "post-pandemic" middle school schedule, dedicates the last period of the day to allow all students to get what they need to catch up or move ahead. Every teacher is available to help, and students seek out or are assigned the support they need.

This is a case where reality seldom matches the good intent. Flex blocks obviously provide extra time (a plus), but this time is rarely used in a way that aligns with best practices: to provide direct, high-quality instruction focused on yet-to-be mastered foundational skills and content. Flex blocks are more often devoted to providing assistance with homework, retaking quizzes, or computer-based independent work.

This approach also falls short in the "expert instruction" area. In a show of commitment to catching kids up, which is admirable, many schools enroll every adult to help during flex block, including PE, art, and world language teachers, for example. These caring staff are unlikely to be content-strong math or reading teachers, which hobbles their ability to teach a concept multiple ways for a student who is struggling with math or struggling to comprehend a complicated text.

Reading across the curriculum. "Every teacher in this school is a reading teacher," the proud and smiling middle school principal shared. "We have embedded reading in every class, including PE, art, math, and so on." In this school and many others like it, all staff teach reading, but that doesn't make them skilled and specially trained reading teachers. Teaching middle school students who struggle to comprehend or read fluently is not easy. Although it is a best practice for all teachers to teach academic vocabulary and to connect their lessons to themes from other classes, teaching a struggling reader requires extensive training. These students need lots of direct instruction from a skilled reading teacher—at least 45 minutes a day, five days a week.

Keys to strategic intervention

The research is clear: students who struggle need extra-time intervention delivered by content-strong staff. At the middle school level, this means providing an extra period of reading, math, or ELA intervention each day. However, this approach requires embracing a few guiding principles.

Restrict extra help. Only students who really need extra help should get extra help. It is unfair and inequitable to have students who don't struggle lose an entire period a day receiving support they do not need.

Go deep, not wide. Allowing students and teachers to focus on intervention in one subject for weeks or months will be more impactful than trying to provide a few minutes of ongoing support across all the subjects a student might struggle with. Middle school students can have low self-esteem. It can be demoralizing to get intervention in three subjects and make little headway in all three because each subject only gets a bit of attention. Conversely, students this age can be energized by making progress in a subject they have long struggled with. After receiving daily intervention in math for nine months, one student shared, "I don't feel stupid anymore. I finally get math!"

Focus on foundational skills. Finding time in the schedule for daily intervention requires prioritizing mastery of reading, English, or math intervention not because of state tests but because students who struggle in these subjects will struggle all through middle school and high school and often after graduation as well. Giving up a semester or year of foreign language or an elective is a small price to pay for a lifetime of benefit.

Set staffing and teaching loads that reflect the importance of content-strong interventionists. Many middle schools embrace grade-level teaching teams consisting of a math, ELA, science, and social studies teacher. This means there is an equal number of each type of teacher, and they each teach an equal number of periods a day. It also means there isn't a content-strong teacher available to teach math intervention, for example. Middle schools that have closed the achievement gap and accelerated learning schedule differently, and they staff differently in two ways.

The first difference is the team will have more than one math teacher, with the second teacher dedicated to teaching intervention classes. Often this intervention math teacher is part of more than one team. The second difference is that in some schools, every math and ELA teacher will also teach an intervention class each day. In the name of fairness, the science and social studies teachers on the team might be asked to teach an elective like forensics or the history of technology.

Extend best-practice intervention to students with special needs. Many students with mild to moderate disabilities who struggle in math, reading, and writing would benefit from the same intervention provided to their nondisabled peers. Gap-closing middle schools write IEPs, when appropriate, that include students with disabilities in the same intervention classes taught by general education staff along with nondisabled students who struggle.

At this point in the chapter, some readers might be feeling uncomfortable, wondering if we are suggesting abandoning the middle school model to embrace more effective intervention. Having visited some of the most successful middle schools in the country, we can say that it's not an either/or situation but a both/and one. The best practices for intervention don't require abandoning the middle school model, but they *do* require scheduling a little differently.

Defining Equity as Giving Each Student What They Need

Like many teachers across the country, middle school staff have been loud and proud advocates in the movement to improve equity. Addressing the needs of historically underserved students is a priority at all levels. Central to improving equity is the oft-stated mantra "Equity isn't the same as equality." Equity demands that every student gets what they need, even when some students need more than others.

This commitment to giving kids what they need, even if it's more or different from what we give their peers, seems to be overlooked when it comes to intervention in many middle schools. When schools schedule double periods of 6th grade ELA, for example, it's a case of equality (everyone gets extra help in English) rather than equity (those who need extra help in English get extra help in English). In conversations with hundreds of middle school teachers and leaders, we have heard the tension between scheduling each student based on their unique needs versus keeping the team together. This might be changing in the aftermath of disrupted learning from the pandemic. More middle schools are differentiating student schedules to provide extra time intervention in the subject most needed by each student and skipping intervention for those who don't need it.

In some middle schools, the needs of one group of students, however, are still sacrificed in the name of equality, rather than equity. Few topics generate as much energetic discussion as accelerated classes in middle school. The idea that some students would take a more advanced course than their peers is hotly debated in some districts.

Those who favor having some accelerated classes note that some kids can master a year's worth of math content in six months or others can and want to learn more math than what's outlined in state grade-level standards. In an era that values giving each student what they need (and trying to increase the number of scientists and engineers), accelerated math, especially in 7th and 8th grades, can be a reasonable option. Not everyone sees it this way.

One superintendent colleague of Nate's joined a new district and immediately promised to end accelerated math in all middle schools. As a trained engineer and lover of math, Nate was surprised by his colleague's passion for stamping out higher-level math classes. When he asked why this was a top priority, the superintendent shared, with vigor and volume, that he saw it as a social justice issue.

Nate pressed him and, in so doing, nearly ended a friendship. "How is eliminating accelerated math in grades 7 and 8 going to make the world a better place?" Nate asked. The superintendent's response was enlightening: "Our low-level math classes are disproportionately Black and Brown students, while accelerated math is overwhelming white. Plus, accelerated students are separated from their nonaccelerated peers all day long. This is wrong, and it won't continue on my watch!"

Nate thought carefully about what to say next. "I agree with both those concerns," he finally said, "but why do you want to end accelerated math?"

"I just told you why," the superintendent replied. But he hadn't.

We fully agree with what this superintendent was objecting to—the two common negative corollaries to having accelerated math in middle school. Let's look at each drawback and at how strategic scheduling can eliminate it.

Inequitable course composition

First, it's true that in diverse schools, lower-level classes are often disproportionately composed of Black and Brown students and accelerated math courses are disproportionally composed of white and Asian American students. This is bad and unjust. It is inequity in full view.

Our first question is why schools or districts offer "lower-level classes" at all. There's no rule stating that courses need to have three levels: *accelerated, grade-level*, and *remedial*. Research tells us clearly that having below-grade-level classes is not a best practice for nearly all students (Schwartz, 2021). Ending lower-level classes is a great idea, but there's no reason to link that to ending accelerated math.

Likewise, the homogeneity of accelerated math courses is not desirable, but fixing the problem of course composition is better than eliminating the class. Schools should and can increase participation in accelerated math by historically marginalized students. Here's how.

Provide effective intervention in the early grades. This increases the odds that more students will be ready for accelerated math.

Don't rely on teacher recommendations for inclusion in accelerated math. Unfortunately, teachers, like all of us, have biases. These can lead to disproportionately selecting white and Asian students for accelerated classes.

Use untimed, objective universal screeners for student placement decisions. The best way to figure out who is ready for accelerated math is to see who has the prerequisite math skills. Some schools have seen dramatic increases in enrollment (and mastery) in accelerated math by historically marginalized students when objective measures of readiness are put in place.

Reach out personally to students who are ready for accelerated math but don't opt in. Often these students feel they don't belong in an accelerated class. A private conversation with a trusted adult can change this perception.

Don't assume grades are a good indicator of content mastery. Too many schools see getting an *A* in 6th grade math as in indicator of mastery and getting a *B–* as the opposite. Some students with a *B–* final grade earned a 95 on the final exam but seldom turned in homework, didn't participate in class, or got a *D* on the team project. These are students who are strong in math but not engaged in their math class. Accelerated math might be exactly what's best for them.

Segregation that extends throughout the school day

One of the worst side effects of having a few sections of accelerated math is that these students tend to travel together to all their other classes. It's not unheard of to see PE classes made up entirely of accelerated math students or having none of these students at all. The same can be true for lunch, with teachers referring to the second lunch period as "accelerated lunch"! None of this is in line with the spirit of the middle school model. Fortunately, it's easily avoided.

Having accelerated math needn't lead to students traveling as a pack the rest of the day. This may surprise some. We have heard from many assistant principals that they so wish they could schedule otherwise, but it can't be done. They say this with the certainty of a physicist acknowledging, "You just can't turn off gravity." If you schedule by hand or aren't a scheduling guru, avoiding this problem does seem impossible. Fortunately, most scheduling software programs have functionality to specifically ensure that students in one class aren't grouped all together again in other classes. A scheduling expert can make this problem go away so the accelerated classes can stay. Another option is to mix noncore classes, such as art, PE, and music, by grade level. Doing so allows schedulers to "spread out" students in accelerated math that otherwise might be clumped together in noncore classes in a single grade.

If the undesired side effects of having accelerated math classes can be mitigated, hopefully the conversation will shift to what's best for each student.

What about "Algebra 1 for all"?

Another solution to the challenge of meeting the needs of middle school students who are ready for more rigorous and faster-paced math instruction seems to be growing in popularity. However, it also seems to prioritize equality over equity. The "Algebra 1 for all" movement essentially says, "Let's accelerate math instruction for all middle school students." In this model, the sequence of math courses is altered such that all 8th grade students take Algebra 1, not just students in the accelerated class.

Though it is desirable that all students be ready and able to master Algebra 1 in 8th grade, it's simply not the case in many schools. This one-size-fits-all approach fails to differentiate course offerings based on what students need. It also has the unintended effect of inhibiting students' success in high school math and discouraging many from pursing STEM careers, which is the exact opposite of the strategy's intent. When a student is placed in a math course that they aren't ready for, they get disillusioned, feel they "aren't good at math," and eventually get tracked into lower-level high school math classes that reinforce their self-image of not being "a math person."

Maximizing the Impact of Teacher Collaboration Time

A hallmark of the middle school model is that grade-level teams often meet daily for "team time." The four core subject teachers plus a special education teacher, a guidance counselor, the assistant principal, and others meet for one period a day to collaborate. As most school business officers know, this requires a significant investment of money as well as time. To allow for daily collaboration while also ensuring that teachers get a prep period each day, middle school core subject staff typically teach four classes a day, while their high school counterparts teach five. In a middle school with 900 students, for example, daily collaboration time increases staffing costs by approximately $750,000 a year. Given the magnitude of the investment, it's important to ensure teacher collaboration is as impactful as possible.

Having joined many grade-level team meetings through the years, we have been impressed by the depth of understanding and care team members have for their students. Each day's discussion often focuses on the needs of a few students, with team members sharing different perspectives on the child's history, family situation, and needs. Then everyone brainstorms how best to help. Most of the conversation focuses on the student's social, emotional, or behavioral needs.

It's less common to hear a conversation about how to improve the teaching of multiplying fractions, lesson planning for next week, or why so many students struggled to find the relevance of *Romeo and Juliet.* Teaching- and learning-focused conversations are the mainstay of teacher collaboration time at the elementary and high school level, but these are much less common in middle schools. It shouldn't be surprising, however. With only one math teacher and one English teacher present, it would be hard to plan a better lesson for multiplying fractions or rethinking the assignment for the unit on Shakespeare.

Students and staff benefit when teacher collaboration time is a mix of grade-level teams and content teams. Some schools, for example, have the math team meet three times a week and the grade-level team just twice a week. Some prioritize content teams through daily department meetings and weekly or monthly grade-level meetings.

The research is compelling that when teachers work together to plan future lessons, review the effectiveness of past lessons, and refine their craft based on student outcomes, both teachers and kids benefit (Reynolds, 2008).

If you are thinking, *Sounds interesting, but it would be impossible to schedule a mix of department and grade-level team meetings,* your school is likely scheduling by hand or lacks an expert scheduler. Most student information systems (SIS) include powerful scheduling software, such as PowerSchool or Infinite Campus, with built-in modules specifically designed for scheduling a mix of grade-level and content-specific planning time. See Chapter 11 for more on the importance of technical scheduling expertise.

The other option that many schools pursue is scheduling an early release or late arrival day once a week, typically on a Wednesday or Friday. Doing so creates an uninterrupted block of time, usually an hour or two, for teachers and staff across grade levels to collaborate in any number of combinations. The instructional time lost in such an approach is often well rewarded when teachers use the planning time effectively. An interesting twist on this approach is called *internal early release.* The kids stay in school, but core classes are canceled. While some teachers meet by department, others head up large-group projects like field days, assemblies, or team building.

Change Is Hard; These Steps Can Help

Changing any schedule is hard, but in our experience, changing a middle school schedule is especially challenging. Often the changes can feel like an attack on the middle school model (it isn't), an undermining of teacher collaboration (it needn't be), and an abandonment of core values (it shouldn't be). We know more than a few superintendents and assistant superintendents for teaching and learning who were vilified or run out of town for trying to create strategic middle school schedules. In most cases, they had the right schedule but the wrong process. Here are our lessons learned, presented as steps of what to do:

1. **Define *equity* at the beginning of the process.** Most teachers embrace equity, but many push back against differentiated intervention or course levels. If a school can agree that equity means every student getting what they need (rather than every student being treated the same), these kinds of changes are more readily embraced.

2. **Get meaningful teacher input.** Gather information over a period of months, not days or weeks. What's working well, what do some students need more time on, and how can every minute be treated as precious? Be sure to reach out to the high school teachers who will be serving these middle school students in just a few years. High school staff have a unique vantage point on how well middle school prepared students for what comes next.

3. **Make sure that all teachers are heard—but that teachers of core subjects aren't underrepresented.** Often a small planning committee of teachers is formed in an effort to represent the various voices within the school. This sounds like good policy, but in practice it can mean a committee composed of one core subject teacher, one arts teacher, one technology teacher, one guidance counselor, and someone from the music department. In pursuit of inclusiveness, core subject teachers might account for just one of six voices around the table. A planning committee that is at least half core subject

teachers more proportionately represents the school's teaching staff. The committee might get a bit larger, but that's OK.

4. **Listen to student voices too.** Through surveys and focus groups, student wants, perspectives, and realities should be brought into the conversation. Inviting a group of students who struggle academically or who excel in math can change the tenor of the discussion of intervention or accelerated math. Gathering input from recent "graduates" of the middle school who are now in high school can also be a powerful and helpful feedback mechanism.

5. **Bring in a scheduling guru.** Too often the best schedules are abandoned because the current scheduler doesn't know how to build a schedule that's strategic and looks very different from current practice. There is no reason to assume anyone in a school is an expert scheduler because very few folks have been provided training. Read more about this in Chapter 11.

6. **Reduce, rather than eliminate.** Saying goodbye to a beloved practice can be jarring. It often generates intense pushback and a huge sense of loss. Reducing a current practice, but not fully eliminating it, can soften the blow and heighten the support. If a school has daily grade-level team meetings, for example, don't eliminate them, but shift some of these to content-specific department meetings. If the school prescribes all noncore classes, initiate student choice over what courses they can take in 8th grade only rather than in all grades.

7. **Take time to plan.** Few schools can revamp a middle school schedule in less than six months, and many need more time. Any planning that results in significant changes to the schedule should begin at least a full year before you intend to implement the new schedule. This means never starting the schedule revamping process in the spring. Too often we get calls asking us to help create a schedule that must be submitted to the central office and shared with staff in two or three weeks' time. Rushed efforts are doomed to create pushback. Given both the importance of schedules and teacher input, it's best to incorporate scheduling discussions into the existing

meeting schedule. Use facility meetings and team meetings to get input on needs and draft schedules. Use PD days or early releases to share scheduling best practices. Avoid after-school meetings because some staff won't be able to participate.

8. **Don't forget that strategic scheduling can affect staffing.** Schedules and staffing are related. Let the schedule drive the staffing plan.

9. **Ensure no current staff loses their job.** Any changes in staffing should be done through attrition.

10. **Make a comprehensive and bold plan, but implement it incrementally.** Often a strategic schedule includes many big changes, sometimes too many to absorb at once. It can be helpful to implement some changes next year, others a year later, and the final improvements a year after that. It's fine to roll out the changes in stages, but it's best to be clear when each change will take effect. One school we helped rethink their schedule committed to big changes but also a phased implementation. In Year 1, they added extra-time intervention. In Year 2, they gave students some choice in grades 7 and 8, and it wasn't until Year 3 that they implemented significant student voice and choice. They used Year 2 to survey students and staff and plan a few new courses.

◆ ◆ ◆

The middle school model has much to offer students of a special age, and thoughtfully constructed strategic schedules can bring out the best in every middle school and every middle schooler. Change is never easy, but it's worth the effort.

The next chapter continues our discussion of middle school schedule but shifts the focus to increasing student engagement.

6

Strategic Scheduling to Increase Middle School Engagement

Heighten student engagement through voice, choice, and time for relationship building

Education is the pathway to becoming an informed citizen and a successful adult. To a 6th, 7th, or 8th grader, however, school can seem boring, lonely, or just plain unimportant. A large Gallup poll revealed that on any given day, nearly half of middle school students are disengaged, feel that their teachers don't care about them, and don't see value in what they are learning (Brenneman, 2016).

Maybe these comments from disengaged students will sound familiar:

- "Why do I need to know what x is anyway?"
- "When will I ever need to know what side Austria was on during World War I . . . and why should I care about Austria at all?!"
- And the saddest comment of all: "No one will even notice if I don't come to school."

Having looked at how strategic scheduling can help schools better meet the academic needs of middle school students, we turn in this chapter to its potential to better support the whole child. Most school and district leaders already know that increasing student engagement increases attendance, motivation, and academic outcomes. What's less common knowledge is that the school schedule can be a big driver of higher student engagement.

Why Middle School Engagement Needs Reconsideration

It's easy to assume that most middle schools do a great job of engaging their students. For starters, being student-centered is the foundation of the middle school model. The concept of grade-level teams (100 or so students sharing the same math, ELA, science, and social studies teachers) and teacher team time (these four teachers and other staff meeting often to coordinate their support of each student) is aligned with the middle school purpose of knowing every child and meeting their individual needs.

Middle schools also invest heavily in the idea that noncore classes—fine and industrial arts, music, and so on—will enrich the overall learning experience and amp up student engagement. As discussed in Chapter 5, this is one reason most middle schools spend less time on core instruction than elementary or high schools do. Preserving time for noncore classes is at the root of most of the resistance we have seen to middle school schedule adjustments aimed at increasing time for intervention ("If kids lose art or music to get extra help, they might stop coming to school completely!")—and this is despite the fact, as we mentioned in the previous chapter, that effective intervention can actually increase student motivation. So do noncore classes, which account for 35–40 percent of every middle school student's day, actually create engagement?

They do, but only if they are the *right* noncore courses. Some middle schools offer a wide, varied, and eclectic set, but many more do not. Their noncore offerings are pretty similar to what Nate had in middle school—and he graduated from middle school in 1974! Wood shop has generally been replaced by a technology course, but the rest are very familiar: art, music, PE, and family/consumer sciences. While both the world and middle school students themselves have changed a lot since the 1970s, there's little evidence of this in typical noncore course offerings. What's more, because these traditional offerings were developed by and for white middle-class teachers and students, they often are not culturally relevant or affirming for students of color. So it should not be too surprising that despite many middle schools' sincere and significant commitment to student engagement, far too many middle schoolers still feel unmotivated and unnoticed.

Three scheduling strategies can turn this situation around and supercharge student engagement: elevating voice, increasing choice, and dedicating time to effective relationship building. All fit squarely into the course offering section of the strategic scheduling framework (see Chapter 1) and align with two of the hallmarks of strategically scheduled middle schools introduced in Chapter 5: engaging students in their passions while giving them the opportunities to discover new ones and creating meaningful bonds between students and staff.

Elevating voice, increasing choice, and dedicating time to relationship building don't cost a dollar more, nor do they require additional staff. They are a practical way to increase your school's commitment to the whole child and to the middle school model. This chapter will explore these strategies and the factors that can contribute to their success or get in the way.

Elevating Student Voice

Elevating student voice means giving students input into what courses are offered. It doesn't mean they get to *choose* which courses they take; that's student *choice*, which we will discuss a bit later.

Many middle schoolers are exploring who they are and who they want to be and wondering what they will become. Their personalities, interests, and passions may still be taking shape but are often put on full display in how they dress, what they watch or listen to, and how they spend their time after school. For noncore courses to be an effective hook that will make kids want to come to school and want to be there, these courses must tap into real student interests and passions. They must be relevant, culturally affirming, and legitimately engaging.

Here are three ways to update and invigorate noncore offerings:

- **Offer new flavors of old favorites.** Art and music, for example, are still very interesting and important, but they can come in many forms. A school can keep the noncore courses it has but update the content and units within those courses.
- **Embrace modern trends.** Lots of today's popular hobbies didn't exist 20 years ago (let alone 10 years ago), so it's not surprising that some new courses are needed.
- **Look to the core.** Many popular noncore classes are spinoffs of content students learn in core classes and can be taught by core-course teachers.

So that's what to do; let's look more closely at how to do it.

Specialize instead of eliminate

Often discussions with middle school staff and leaders about giving students greater voice causes anxiety. Fears that art, music, and PE "aren't relevant to students today" will typically stop these conversations before they get very far. Fear not. When students have a say, they often say they *want* art, music, and PE—just not necessarily the art, music, and PE of the past.

One middle school we worked with had a typical set of noncore offerings, including Art 6, 7, and 8; Music 6, 7, and 8; and PE 6, 7, and 8. As the names suggest, these were generic courses that covered a range of art projects, genres of music, and physical activities. The exact curricular makeup of the classes varied by teacher and was frequently a mystery to the students. It's hard to say a course will keep kids motivated to come to school when they don't even know what topics will be covered or what they will be doing.

If you ask students this age if they like art, or if art excites them, many will say it does. Seldom, however, will a student tell you, "I love Art 6!" Instead, they'll tell you they love learning to use photo editing tools, drawing graphic novels, making jewelry, shooting and editing movies, designing websites, composing and playing music, and so on. So, if student interests are specific and focused, it makes sense that adding specificity and focus is a good way to morph traditional noncore classes into more engaging versions of themselves. In music, for example, this might mean a move from a generic survey course to a music course focused on specialty areas that students say interest them the most—Electronic Music, World Music, and DJing. Similarly, the traditional PE class might become Yoga, Free Weights, or Barre if student surveys suggest these are their preferred forms of exercise.

Considering the ways in which technology has infused itself into traditional disciplines can also guide your updating efforts. Today, more professional artists draw on a tablet made by Apple or Microsoft than a tablet made of paper or canvas. For many students, art is digital, not physical; they create "watercolors" and "charcoal drawings" with a computer program. Music has also become entwined with technology. In one district, many students wanted to produce music electronically in a sound studio with a synthesizer rather than sing or play an instrument.

Here are some examples of old favorites presented in new flavors:

- **Art:** Animation Workshop, Art and Design in Theatre, Art History, Calligraphy, Ceramics, Fashion Design, Film Analysis, Graphic Design, Interior Design, Video Production
- **Music:** Evolution of American Music, Exploration of Music, Guitar, Hip Hop History, Intro to Pop Music, Mariachi Band, Music Production, World Music
- **Health and PE:** Mind-Body Wellness, Nutrition, Personal Fitness, Stress Management, Yoga, Weightlifting

Keep up with the times

Thirty years ago, very few people watched TV shows about cooking. Today, *The Great British Baking Show, Top Chef,* and many more crowd the airwaves. Being a foodie is a form of self-identification that didn't exist back in the day. Similarly, *entrepreneurship* used to mean going door to door selling lightbulbs; today, it's about pitching new product ideas, as seen on *Shark Tank.* Sports have evolved as well, with new events continually being added to and subtracted from the Olympic Games and the X-Games drawing young viewers from around the world.

The gap between today's student areas of interest and middle school course offerings can be very wide. Wouldn't it be great if kids didn't have to wait to get home to engage in what excites them the most? Just look to what students do in their free time—including the games and sports they play, what they read, what they watch on TV or online, and who they follow on social media—and their interests will become clearer.

Here is a sample of some of the newer noncore elective offerings we've seen in middle schools:

- **STEM:** Animal Science: The Pet Vet, App Design, Architecture, Astronomy, Challenge Math, Chemistry Creations, Computer Skills and Application, Digital Media, Engineering, Environmental Ecology, Game Design, Myth Busters, Problem-Solving Games, Robotics
- **Interdisciplinary:** Apocalyptic Survival, Broadcast Media, Career Awareness, Chess, Community Action, Contemporary Issues, Shark Tank, Leadership, Personal Finance, The Stock Market, Speech and Debate, Youth and the Law
- **Dance and Theater Arts:** Ballet, Choreography, Contemporary Dance, Hip Hop Dance, Improv, Intro to Dance: Jazz & Tap, Introduction to Acting, Modern Dance, Shakespeare

Explore core course spin-offs

When most educators discuss programming to engage students, they often assume it's the unified arts that have the most appeal. But topics in English, math, science, and social studies can be engaging electives too. Based on surveys we've conducted students throughout the country, it's clear that some of the most sought-after courses could be taught by core subject teachers you already have on staff.

When middle school students are asked questions like "What do you *want* to learn more about?" or "What do you read and discuss with your friends outside school?" often their answers are very specific aspects of core subjects—but aspects that aren't discussed in much detail during the core class. For example, many students want to read, write, and discuss science fiction. A course called Post-Apocalyptic Sci-Fi would likely have many interested students. Racial justice and current events also score high on the interest scale of many middle schoolers. In one district, the most requested elective was a science class on Stephen Hawking's explanation of the big bang and the birth of the universe; in second place was a course called Einstein for Beginners.

Here are a few more examples of elective courses that might be taught by core subject teachers:

- **Fantasy Sports Math:** Students use statistical data and basic math to run their own fantasy sports teams.
- **Podcasting 101:** Students learn the steps to write, produce, and post their own podcast, drawing on the lessons and structure taught by an English teacher.
- **Myth Busters:** Students use the scientific method to investigate claims, both common and unusual. Students also watch episodes of the TV show *Myth-Busters* for inspiration and to analyze and critique the investigative methods demonstrated on the show.
- **Race and Social Justice in the United States:** Students examine issues of race, inequality, and social justice in modern U.S. society and discuss ways to address these challenges.

A welcoming environment. Core subject-related courses are also a way to bring some aspects of equity into the curriculum. Offering a course on race and social justice is a direct way, but so is something like offering a course on great authors from the home nation of the school's largest group of English language learners or from a country to which a significant portion of students have cultural ties. Ideally, culturally relevant content should also be woven into core course lessons, but dedicating space in noncore courses also says, "We know you are here, and we value your history and culture." At the end of this chapter, we provide a step-by-step process you can use to survey students and staff for potential new courses along with sample surveys to use as models.

The budget benefits. The focus of this chapter is first and foremost student engagement and student learning, but offering core subject-related elective courses taught by core subject teachers can be great for the budget as well. We cover this topic in greater detail in Chapter 10, but let's take a quick look now.

It's easiest to make this approach cost-effective in middle schools where math, science, English, and social studies teachers have (or could have) an extra teaching block available each day. They might currently teach four periods of a seven-period school day. If middle school teachers taught an elective as a fifth period, no additional staffing would be needed to offer, say, Current Events, The Big Bang, or The Math of Fantasy Sports.

There are middle schools in which core subject teachers can teach no more than four periods a day, as detailed in their collective bargaining agreement. A look at their schedules suggests they are booked solid. In some instances, they are, but this needn't be the case. We can illustrate this point best through a couple of scenarios.

Assume there are 100 students in grade 8, and the school uses a teaming model (one core subject teacher per team). In this scenario, Teacher A teaches four periods of Social Studies 8, with 25 students in each class, and has one period every day blocked out for team planning with colleagues. There is no open spot in Teacher A's schedule to pick up another (elective) course. This teacher is at full capacity.

Now assume there are 75 students in grade 8—a slightly smaller enrollment. The school uses the same kind of teaming model described above and has the same schedule. In this scenario, Social Studies Teacher B teaches four periods of Social Studies 8, with 19 students in each class, and spends the remaining period in team planning. Teacher B's schedule is full, just like Teacher A's, but is Teacher B really at full capacity?

Figure 6.1 shows what's possible if these 75 students were redistributed, shifted from four classes of 19 into three classes of 25. Teacher B would teach the same number of students overall, and all three classes would be in line with district class-size norms. But Teacher B would now be available to teach a new elective related to social studies—a course in current events, perhaps, or racial justice—that could be offered at no additional cost. The same would be true for the other three teachers on Teacher B's grade-level team.

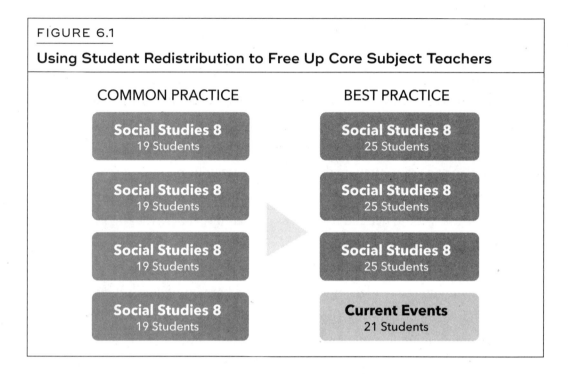

FIGURE 6.1

Using Student Redistribution to Free Up Core Subject Teachers

COMMON PRACTICE

Social Studies 8
19 Students

Social Studies 8
19 Students

Social Studies 8
19 Students

Social Studies 8
19 Students

BEST PRACTICE

Social Studies 8
25 Students

Social Studies 8
25 Students

Social Studies 8
25 Students

Current Events
21 Students

Connect middle school noncore courses to high school offerings

When middle schools sit down to debate and plan noncore course offerings, a lot of folks want to join the discussion. One person who is seldom invited is a high school principal or guidance counselor. Why should they be at the table? Because every middle schooler becomes a high school student later. Connecting middle school non-core course offerings to high school course offerings is a smart way to help kids.

Middle schoolers might be less inclined to develop skills in an area if they can't continue to develop those skills throughout the rest of their school career. For example, in one district we worked with, the middle school offered Guitar (an excellent elective!) to 7th and 8th graders; the high school had no such offering. As the teacher of this course remarked, "With no option for students to continue their interest in guitar, it's a weird, dead-end course. It's hard to motivate students when they know there is no option in high school for them to continue after my course." Simply listing out elective offerings at both the middle school and high school can be an effective way to quickly discern where pathways to pursue interests between grade levels already exist and where gaps or dead ends may need to be addressed.

Also, some great high school electives might be undersubscribed because students never got a chance to taste them before having to commit to a year-long class. This is especially true when it comes to career technical education (CTE) and career pathways. Middle school students think a lot about what they might "be in the future," and interest in career exploration is high during 7th and 8th grade. In districts with academy-style high schools based on career pathways, allowing students to test the waters in middle school can lead to far better decisions in high school and beyond.

Just ask

The easiest way to learn what interests students is to just ask them. A student voice survey is simple to administer but can be hard to write—often because many students are skeptical that their input will change course offerings and self-censor from the start. When asked an open-ended question like "What would you like to see changed in noncore classes, such as music or art?" they will often just suggest tweaks to existing courses. So they might reply, "I wish music was a bit more up-to-date," when what they really want to say is "I'd love classes in hip-hop or on music as a vehicle for social justice." Unless prompted, many students, like many adults, also won't consider core subject-related electives, such as Science Fiction. The possibility of courses like Entrepreneurship or Shark Tank probably isn't even on their radar.

A multi-step survey process, outlined in Figure 6.2, is usually best. Step 1 is an interest survey designed to draw out what excites kids. Step 2 involves reaching out to teachers to try to match high-interest topics with teacher expertise. And then it's back to students for Step 3, a follow-up survey that reframes what the first survey has revealed and asks students to rank their interest in potential new courses. Some courses will need short descriptions to help students make an informed choice. A few schools interview recent 8th grade graduates, who have a very full picture of the current offerings and how they did or didn't match their interests.

FIGURE 6.2

How to Learn What Your Students Find Engaging

Overview

Creating middle school noncore offerings based on student interest is a three-step process. What follows is a suggested guide for providing students greater voice. It is just a sample and should be modified to reflect your community.

Step 1: Collect Student Interest Data

The first step is to determine, broadly speaking, what your students are interested in learning and what their passions are. This calls for questions that are broad and general in nature.

A Sample Student Interest Survey

Our school is committed to offering interesting and engaging classes for all our students. As part of this commitment, we want to learn more about your interests, hobbies, and passions—both at school and beyond school. **The purpose of this survey is to gather information that will help us create new courses for you and your fellow students.** After you complete this survey, the teachers and leaders of the school will create a menu of possible new courses. We will survey you once again to learn which courses are of the most interest to you. Please complete this survey by _____. Your opinion matters!

1. **What activities do you most enjoy outside school?** (Examples might be *playing sports, cooking, dancing, building models,* etc.)
2. **What are your hobbies?**
3. **What types of books do you like to read for fun?** (Examples might be *science fiction, graphic novels,* stories set in a particular time or place or culture, etc.)
4. **What topics do you follow on social media?** (Examples might be *beauty, extreme sports, e-games,* etc.)
5. **What are your favorite things to watch on TV?** (Examples might be *Shark Tank, The Great British Baking Show, Stranger Things, NFL football,* etc.)
6. **What is your favorite kind of art?** (Examples might be *photography, drawing, sculpture,* etc.)
7. **What are your favorite types of music to listen to?**
8. **What are your favorite forms of physical activity?** (Examples might be *yoga, working out at a gym, basketball, running,* etc.)
9. **What topics in current events or politics you would like to learn more about?**
10. **If our school added one new course, what would you like it to be?**

Step 2: Collect Information from Teachers

With the understanding gained from Step 1, gauge teachers' interest, expertise, and willingness to teach potential new course offerings.

A Sample Teacher Survey

As part of our commitment to provide greater voice to our students, which we believe will increase their engagement and attendance, we recently surveyed them on their interests, hobbies, and passions. A summary of what they shared is included at the end of this survey. As you will see, some of their feedback builds directly from our current offerings but specializes a bit (focusing on one aspect of art, PE, music, etc.). Some of their interests touch on topics we don't currently address in existing courses. The next step in this process is to learn what topics our staff would be interested in teaching and begin brainstorming how this interest can be structured into a class. Please complete the enclosed survey of staff interests. **The purpose of this survey is to determine where student and staff passions overlap.**

Please refer to the summary of student interests to answer the following questions.

1. **Which hobbies, interests, or passions do you share with the students?**
2. **Which of these shared hobbies, interests, or passions might lend themselves to a new course offering that you would potentially be interested in teaching?**
3. **What support would you need to create and offer this new course?**
4. **If there was just one new course for our students, what do you think it should be?**
5. **Are there any other thoughts you want to share to help us provide greater voice to our students?**

Step 3: Gauge Student Interest in Potential New Courses

With a sense of how student and teacher interests align, create and share with students a list of specific potential new courses and ask them to rank their preferences. It is this ranked list that you should ultimately use to inform new course creation.

Sample Possible New Course Interest Survey

Our school is committed to offering interesting and engaging classes for all our students. As part of this commitment. we previously asked you about your interests, hobbies, and passions. Since then, we have analyzed your answers, discussed them with all the teachers, and generated a list of POSSIBLE new courses. Not all of these courses will be offered because the list of potentials is very long, reflecting the many and varied interests of you and your classmates. **The purpose of this survey is to help us prioritize the possible new courses**. Please complete this survey by _____. Your opinion matters!

FIGURE 6.2

How to Learn What Your Students Find Engaging (*continued*)

If the school added a new course in the arts, what are your top 2 choices from the list below? Write #1 by your first choice and #2 by your second choice.

* Insert list of possible new art courses

2. **If the school added a new course in PE, health, and wellness, what are your top 2 choices from the list below?** Write #1 by your first choice and #2 by your second choice.

   * Insert list of possible new PE, health, and wellness courses

3. **If the school added a new course in music or performing arts, what are your top 2 choices from the list below?** Write #1 by your first choice and a #2 by your second choice.

   * Insert list of possible new music or performing arts courses

4. **If the school added other new courses, what are your top 2 choices from the list below?** Write #1 by your first choice and #2 by your second choice.

   * Insert list of all other possible courses

5. **Given all the choices, what are the three courses you would be most interested in taking?** List them in order below.

6. **What current course that you take—other than math, English, science or social studies—would you be willing to give up so that you could take a new course?** Write it below.

Providing Student Choice

Student voice and student choice often go together, but they are two separate discussions and decisions. *Voice* gives students input over what courses are offered. *Choice* gives students the ability to select what courses they take from a menu. If they helped create the menu, then there is both voice and choice. If they didn't, then there is only choice.

Why choice is important

Even with increased voice, few offerings will excite all students. Just consider how students dress, how they decorate the inside of their lockers, what they watch on YouTube, or the stories they share with friends on Monday morning, and it's obvious that their interests are diverse.

After working with thousands of secondary school teachers and leaders, it's fascinating how differently most high schools think about choice compared to middle schools. High schools nearly universally embrace high levels of student choice. Their thinking is if students learn more about topics that interest them, they will be more engaged, more excited by school, and more likely to retain skills and knowledge. In fact, student choice is so deeply ingrained in most high school cultures that they never even think of not having it.

Middle schools are different. In our experience, most students want choice, and the central office is generally supportive, but many teachers and school leaders are less certain. Here's a look at some of the common concerns they share:

- "Kids need to be exposed to all the arts. I would feel terrible if a student didn't take any art course while in middle school."
- "Middle schoolers are too young to know what their interests are. How can they know if they like music if they never take it?"
- "It's our job to give students a well-rounded education—it's more about breadth than depth at this point."

These are all legitimate perspectives, but other teachers make compelling counterpoints:

- "We need to remember that our students have already taken six years of art and music in elementary school. They have been exposed to many things inside and outside school and do have a sense of what interests them."
- "What is our job really about? Don't we want kids excited to come to school? Making them take an elective class they don't like, or offering an elective course very few want, doesn't seem right to me."

We have watched this kind of discussion go on for months, and often folks on each side dig in. Fortunately, there are options that can mitigate the concerns.

Choice doesn't have to be full choice

Like the name suggests, with *full choice*, students pick their elective classes from a menu that is set by the school leadership. This might be too much freedom for some middle schools.

Bounded choice can be a great compromise. This option mirrors the approach many liberal arts colleges use. They too want well-rounded students, but they also want highly engaged learners. With bounded choice, students are required to sample all the disciplines but still have a lot of autonomy. For example, they might be required to take one art course, one music course, and one PE course each year, but within each of these areas, they can choose from a number of options. The art course could be Watercolors, Digital Art, or Art as Social Protest (taught by a social studies teacher). The PE course might be Basketball or Yoga or Free Weights.

Scaled choice is another popular middle ground. This approach mandates exposure to a predetermined set of topics but gives students more power to choose for themselves as they proceed through middle school. In 6th grade, all students rotate through a set of exploratory courses in art, music, PE, and so on. It's a year supercharged with exploration, especially if the noncore courses are semester-length or even just a quarter long. Rather than having a full year of art, PE, and music, 6th graders could have six semester-long courses or even 12 quarter-long courses, thus sampling a broad array of topics. In 7th grade, some noncore classes are required while others are electives; students are free to explore some new topics that specifically interest them while deepening their understanding of certain topics that the school sees as priorities. In 8th grade, students have full choice over the noncore courses they take.

The debate about choice or no choice often centers on well-rounded versus engaged students. What is seldom discussed is that some kids really, really, *really* dislike some subjects. One district found that more than 10 percent of chronically absent students skipped school to avoid what they saw as the unbearable experience of PE. To share a personal experience, Nate was a good student but extremely self-conscious of his speech impediment. Music class was a living hell for him because he found singing very challenging. His stomach turned just thinking about it.

Middle school is an awkward time. We know this. Student choice can help mitigate some teenage anxiety and make these years a little easier and perhaps a lot more enjoyable.

Is staffing for voice and choice an obstacle or an opportunity?

The hope for giving student voice and choice is often dashed on the rocks of staffing concerns. What if kids want to take The Big Bang or Shark Tank but you don't have staff with availability in their schedule who are prepared to teach these courses? In the short run, the answer is don't offer these courses! Giving students voice doesn't mean they have complete say; yes, they provide input, but school leaders always make the final call. Schools that embrace voice and choice offer noncore classes that kids want to take and that staff want to teach.

After getting input from students through the student interest survey, ask teachers where their interests lie as well. When there is an overlap between teacher passion and student interest, everyone wins.

A more vexing staffing issue, one that is often whispered rather than discussed in the open, needs to be addressed head-on. We appreciate the clear and honest way one art teacher summed up the situation: "While I think it would be great for our students to have some voice and choice in what classes they take, I can't support it. I don't want to be in the business of marketing my class to students and competing against other teachers for students."

Why is this kind of competition unsettling? The worry is that if only half the students sign up for music, then half the music staff will be let go. If staffing is adjusted every year based on student course selections, then no one would ever have job security. This legitimate concern can be easily addressed with a simple no reduction-in-force (RIF) rule. Most schools moving toward student choice commit to never letting a teacher go based on student class selection or offerings. When a vacancy naturally occurs, schools can take into account what courses are oversubscribed or not offered yet but desired.

If offering choice, schools must be prepared to adjust staffing *over time* through attrition to better match student interest. One district had a wide range of electives, and kids had a lot of freedom to learn about what interested them. Well, only some kids did; every year, a few electives were dramatically over-requested. For example, 200 students wanted to take Digital Art, but only 75 seats were available. Nothing is less engaging than asking students what courses they want to take and then not allowing them to enroll. Excitement turns to frustration, especially for students who are placed instead in a class of little interest to them. Over time, course offerings, student interest, and staffing should align.

But is it really possible to schedule with both voice *and* choice?

Even strong advocates for increased engagement through student voice and choice like the idea in concept but are worried about its reality. "Won't this be very hard, maybe even impossible, to schedule?" they wonder. The answer is a resounding yes and no; it's hard for some people but very easy for others. Chapter 11 will dive deeper into the role of the scheduler, but let's touch on a few relevant points here.

It's easier to create a schedule *without* voice and choice. Many middle school guidance counselors or assistant principals know how to build these schedules, and for some of these folks, a full-throated voice and choice schedule would be hard to build. But they can learn, and the good news is that most districts already own the kind of software that makes building complex schedules much easier: PowerSchool, Infinite Campus, and the like. Almost 100 percent of high schools use such scheduling software; middle school staff can be trained to use it as well.

A skilled scheduler armed with good software and the necessary staffing and student interest information can build even the most complex middle school schedule in about three days. In short: being worried about who will build the schedule or how they will do it shouldn't be an obstacle to student voice and choice.

Even with the best software, however, it is easier and more efficient if choice electives serve students from multiple grades. Mixing 7th and 8th graders in a single section of Jewelry Making can be good for socialization, teacher utilization, and efficient staffing. It can be costly to offer this course at three separate grades or if only a handful of students in one grade want it. Multi-age electives require less staffing and are easier to maintain at target class sizes. For many middle schools, this would be an adjustment; typically, noncore courses are all single grade.

Ensuring Time for Relationship Building

Voice and choice can be powerful drivers of student engagement, but neither is as powerful as authentic relationships between students and staff. As the U.S. Centers for Disease Control and Prevention (CDC) have made clear, students who feel connected to their school and teachers are also more likely to have higher academic achievement, including higher grades and test scores; have better school attendance; and stay in school longer (CDC, 2019). And though few kids look back as an adult and say, "Art 7 really changed my life!" many do say their art teacher made a lasting impact. Even when kids say they really like math this year, often it's the math teacher's personalized attention and the relationship they had with the teacher that made the subject stand out.

Nearly all middle schools value student–teacher relationships, but far too many students report that authentic relationships are lacking—despite students spending more than 1,000 hours with their teachers over a typical school year. Middle school, especially, is a time when students tend to be sensitive to social challenges, and self-esteem can be fragile. Longitudinal research has shown that peer-related loneliness is highest and felt most deeply among early adolescents (Ladd & Ettekal, 2013). Strategic scheduling can change this for the better.

The middle school model was designed specifically to create a student-centric climate. It does, but it only goes so far. Working in teaching teams, sharing the same 100 or so students, and meeting daily to discuss what they are seeing from their students do help teachers know more about their students' academic strengths and behavioral challenges. However, this model falls short in terms of helping kids to get to know their teachers. More important, our interviews with students reveal that many want their teachers to know them as *people*, not *students*. What's the difference? Students tell us that when a teachers knows their academic strengths and skill gaps (e.g., "I'm good with fractions but struggle to find the theme of a story"), that's just a teacher doing their job. "Teachers care about learning and maybe state test scores," they reason, "but they don't really care about *me*."

Knowing a student as a person means knowing what they do after school, who their friends are, what they worry about, and what interests them the most. The middle school team model wasn't specifically designed for this.

Advisory to the rescue?

Again, the answer is a resounding *yes and no*. Advisory can be a powerful tool to build authentic student–teacher relationships, which in turn increases student engagement and learning and life outcomes. Advisory periods are sound in theory; however, their implementation frequently comes up short. Strategic scheduling can bridge the gap.

To best understand how smarter schedules can lead to a more effective advisory period, let's start with what makes for effective advisory. To build authentic relationships, for teachers to know each student as a person, and for kids to believe their teacher cares about them, advisory must do the following:

- **Pair students and staff with common interests.** It's not coincidental that nearly all of David's friends enjoy hiking, like he does. Relationships form around shared interests.
- **Avoid previously strained relationships.** It's hard to build a friendship with frustration or animosity as its foundation.
- **Keep the groups small.** Relationships are a one-to-one effort. *Groups* don't form authentic relationships; *individuals* do.
- **Incorporate structured and meaningful activity.** Most friendships are formed while the parties involved are doing something.
- **Prioritize quality of time over quantity.** More isn't better. Better is better.

These five best practices aren't hard to grasp and are seldom controversial. What they are, however, is hard to schedule in the typical middle school.

More often than not, middle school advisory is structured like just another class. Twenty-five kids are assigned to a room, often their homeroom. They meet every day or every other day, opposite a noncore class or intervention block. The teacher is asked to build relationships while the kids sit at their desks. This prototypical advisory doesn't meet any of the best practices, but it was very easy to schedule.

A far better plan would allow students to select which adult they want to have advisory with. It would involve staff sharing their hobbies and interests so that students can look for commonalities or something they find intriguing. In one school we worked with, students were shocked to learn that a math teacher was a master cake decorator and an English teacher was a champion marathoner. Kids who didn't like math or English but loved baking or running rushed to be in advisory with them.

Choosing their advisory leader allowed students to avoid teachers with whom they had friction, both real and imagined. It's hard to open up to an adult that gave you a detention, an *F*, or "disrespected" you. Those teachers might have been in the right, but it's the students' perception that matters in this situation.

It's interesting that when kids are permitted to select advisors. they often go beyond core subject teachers or teachers, period. In one school, the head of maintenance and the head of food service were two of the most requested advisors. One was a former star athlete and the other, a gourmet foodie. If you're willing to engage all available adults as advisors, advisory can drop to a dozen kids per class.

Finally, what to do during advisory matters as much as who is in the room. Middle school is a socially awkward age. Sitting at a desk in a circle with classmates and an adult with the goal of building authentic relationships by talking about yourself can be the height of awkwardness. It can be more anxiety-inducing than calming. Again, the most effective way to build authentic relationships is to interact authentically with someone around shared interests. A concrete way to make this happen is to recast advisory into during-the-day clubs, much like the kind of clubs long held after school. In this approach, the adult advisors share topics that interest them, and kids might sign up for LEGO Robotics, focused discussion groups (long-distance running, the most recent season of *The Great British Baking Show*, or a chance to make medieval tools using only medieval tools—yes, we know of a school that offered this, and it had a small but intense following). Relationships grow organically while people are engaged in a shared interest.

If after-school clubs during the school day is a step too far for your school, consider the middle-ground move of providing advisory teachers with a set of activities that actively engage students. Too many schools assume advisory teachers will just know what to do. They care about kids and want to build a relationship with them, so they will do that. But caring and good intentions don't necessarily translate into being skilled at facilitating a group "get to know you" discussion or having enough time to properly prepare for advisory. Schools that ask a lot of teachers during advisory must either carve out time for collaborative preparation or provide significant guidance, structure, and materials for all advisory teachers to use and reference.

Some teachers think advisory is a time for kids to talk and share, but relationships are a two-way street. Students react well when adults talk candidly about their lives outside the classroom. Creating structured activities—essentially, advisory lesson plans—can help teachers connect to kids.

These best-practice strategies provide the structures to quickly start to build relationships. One period a week of best-practice advisory will be more effective than 45 minutes a day of typical advisory. One district with six middle schools so valued advisory they dedicated a period a day, the equivalent of 28 entire days a year, to it, but left it teachers to figure out what to do. Over time, the period devolved into a study hall, underutilizing time that could have been used for electives, longer core subject classes, or more intervention.

Best-practice advisory is very effective but can be hard to schedule if students are choosing their adviser or area of common interest. But it's not nearly as hard for a skilled scheduler using low-cost or free software. Just like scheduling student choice for electives, effective advisory requires a skilled scheduler. It's requisite but shouldn't be an obstacle.

Whatever strategy you use, it's critical to assess the impact. Only kids can tell you if they believe someone cares about them as a person. Too often principals and others visit advisory classrooms and comment to themselves how well things are going. They see students interacting with adults. It all looks good, but what are the quiet kids thinking? What are the disengaged students feeling? The only way to know is to confidentially survey them. Ask and they will tell.

If you're thinking, "Great idea—we should craft a survey to gauge whether students feel connected to an adult and if school matters to them," just wait. Most schools we work with already have climate surveys or SEL universal screeners with questions that get at these issues. Though most schools survey their students, far fewer use the data to evaluate their relationship-building efforts. This is a lost opportunity.

◆ ◆ ◆

Middle school students are in an age of discovery that is both exciting and scary for them. Voice, choice, and time for authentic relationship building can help expand exploration of interests and reduce anxiety. Strategic schedules help to make this possible.

The next step toward developing a strategic middle school schedule is to complete the self-assessment in Appendix B (see p. 201). It will help you take stock of your current schedule and identify how well it's set up to align with all the best practices we have highlighted.

High School

7

Choosing a High School Schedule Model

Find the best match aligned to your priorities

In the introduction to *How to Prepare the Schedule for a Secondary School*, a book published in 1944 by Harvard University Press, author Leo Ivok of Worcester, Massachusetts, explains that

> The making of a daily schedule or time-table for their schools is a task which few administrators approach with pleasure. Scheduling-making is ordinarily one of the more tedious tasks confronting the secondary-school administrator. The methods which are generally used involve the manipulation of numerous colored tabs, bits of paper, and other paraphernalia, all of which frequently confuse rather than aid in the solution of what would in theory to be an essentially simple problem. (p. 1)

Replace "colored tabs" with "colored sticky notes" and this nearly 80-year-old description of schedule construction would still be accurate for a fair number of schools.

The good news for schedulers in the 21st century is that while high school schedules *are* complex, sophisticated software (any version of which would amaze Mr. Ivok) exists to speed up the process. But even powerful software does not automatically lead to a strategic schedule that raises achievement, deploys talented staff thoughtfully, and does both in a way that is cost-effective. Scheduling software will help you schedule just about anything, but the hard part is still up to you: knowing *what* to schedule and moving beyond the familiar to build a schedule that improves opportunities and outcomes for students.

The Expected Discussion You Will Not Be Getting (and What You'll Get Instead)

Now, if you picked up this book and turned straight to this chapter on high school schedules, you might be expecting a lengthy discussion of the perennially debated question "What is the best schedule model for high schools?" If you read Chapter 2, you already know what the research says: that this is the wrong question to ask. Designing a strategic schedule is less about finding the perfect model and more about being clear on *what* to schedule within any type of schedule model. Be that as it may, we know school and district leaders are always interested to learn more about the benefits and drawbacks of different schedule models, especially at the high school level.

There are many books on school schedules that provide deep, technical explorations of different schedule models and are filled with headache-inducing charts and rows of staffing figures. That is not this chapter (nor is it this book). Our purpose here is to provide a general overview of four popular schedule models and highlight how each may or may not work well for your high school and its staff and students. Those models are (1) the traditional six-, seven-, or eight-period schedule; (2) the A/B block schedule; (3) the rotational drop schedule; and (4) the trimester schedule.

Do these four represent the full universe of schedule models? Certainly not, but we think they are a foundational set of options any high school can consider, riff off, and make their own.

The Traditional Six-, Seven-, or Eight-Period Schedule

In this model, the schedule runs for six, seven, or eight periods a day. Typically, each period lasts 45 to 55 minutes with a few minutes of transition time between each period. Classes might run the full length of the school year, a semester, or a quarter. Figure 7.1 maps a straightforward and very traditional seven-period schedule.

When it's a good choice

Consider the traditional schedule model if your priorities include the following:

- **Simplicity and consistency.** This is the simplest, most consistent schedule model available. Students see the same teachers at the same time every day. It passes what we call the "wake-up test": when students (or teachers) wake up in the morning, they instantly know what their schedule for the day ahead is and do not have to refer to a printed schedule or planner to remember. The model is easily understood by students, staff, families, and external partners.
- **External partnerships.** Schools with many students that engage with the community during the school day (e.g., jobs, internships, community college courses, service opportunities, etc.) prefer this schedule because it is relatively easy to coordinate with outside organizations.

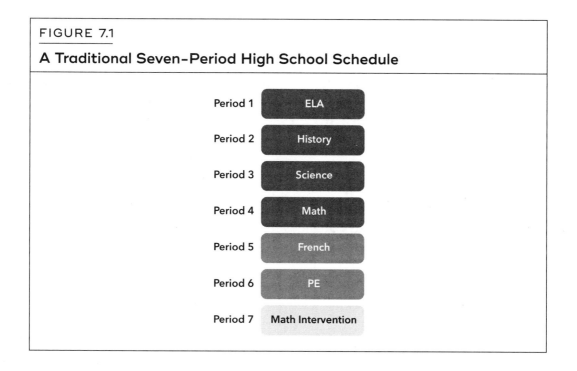

FIGURE 7.1

A Traditional Seven-Period High School Schedule

Period 1	ELA
Period 2	History
Period 3	Science
Period 4	Math
Period 5	French
Period 6	PE
Period 7	Math Intervention

- **Accommodating a high number of shared or part-time teachers.** The consistency of this model makes it relatively friendly to schools with a lot of shared or part-time teachers on staff. A part-time 9th grade English teacher, for example, could teach periods 1 through 3 every day in this model and not have to worry about whether it is an "A-Day" or a "B-Day" (as is the case in an A/B block schedule) or only teach some days of the week (as is the case in a rotational drop schedule).

- **Maximizing core instructional time.** The six- or seven-period version of this model maximizes the percent of a student's day devoted to core instruction. If we assume a student takes four core courses at any given time (math, science, ELA, history), then either 67 percent of their day in a six-period schedule or 57 percent of their day in a seven-period schedule is devoted to core instruction.

- **Offering a high number of singleton courses.** The seven- or eight-period version of this schedule is especially friendly to scheduling a high number of singleton courses, or courses in which only one section of the course runs. For example, if a school only runs one section of AP Chemistry, this would be known as a "singleton." The greater the number of periods in a day, the greater the number of "slots" there are available to schedule courses, and the more flexibility a scheduler has to fit everything in.

Why it might not be best for you

Here are the potential challenges of the traditional schedule to watch out for:

- **Having many periods every day can be draining.** In this schedule model, the attention of teachers and students is spread across many subjects every day. Teachers work with more students at a given time, and students are required to keep a lot of academic balls in the air.

- **Shorter periods may limit instructional methods.** Even the most talented of teachers can only do so much in a 42-minute period, which is common in an eight-period schedule. The more periods in a day, the shorter each instructional period becomes.

- **More periods result in more time lost to transition.** The more periods in the schedule, the more time is shaved off instruction for transition time. Additionally, many and frequent transitions may be challenging for some students.

Six, seven, or eight periods?

Although we believe firmly that no one schedule model is always best, if you were to corner one of us in a dark alley and *insist* we answer the question, the schedule model we think provides high schools with the most strategic mix of flexibility, time on core instruction, efficient use of staff, and student access to a variety of opportunities is a traditional seven-period schedule. A six-period schedule limits the number of courses a student can take in their high school career. An eight-period schedule slices up the day too much; shortens core instruction; and, unless the school is dedicated to new course development, often results in 11th and 12th graders "running out" of courses to take. A seven-period schedule offers an effective balance of variety, efficiency, and simplicity.

The A/B Block Schedule

The A/B block schedule typically divides eight blocks of classes between two alternating days so that students only take four courses a day. Under the A/B schedule, classes last 75–90 minutes and typically run a full year or a full semester.

A variant of this model that adds a bit more flexibility is growing in popularity. It involves splitting one block into two "skinny" periods so that some courses are shorter and more courses can be offered in a week. Figure 7.2 shows an example.

When it's a good choice

Consider the A/B block schedule model if your priorities include the following:

- **A lot of time for varied instruction.** Longer class periods allow for more varied instructional methods and greater depth of material in a given lesson. For this reason, science teachers and performing arts teachers tend to love teaching in a block schedule.

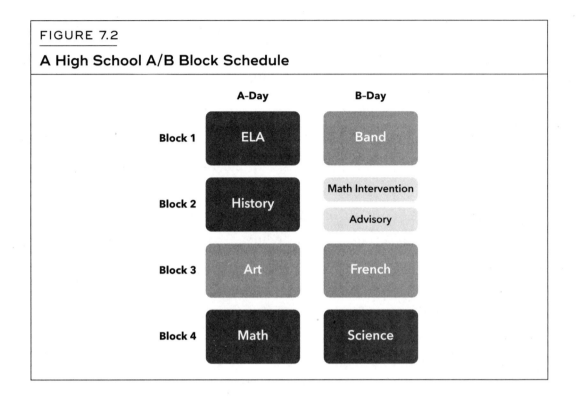

FIGURE 7.2

A High School A/B Block Schedule

- **Maximizing daily time on instruction.** With only three, four, or five periods per day, this model allows schools to reduce transition time and therefore maximize the amount of an *individual school day* spent on instruction. Students typically receive less total time per class over the course of the year, however, than a traditional six- or seven-period schedule model.

- **Minimizing the number of classes students and teachers have on any given day.** Students and teachers only have to focus on four classes per day instead of six or seven (or eight). Teachers also benefit from teaching one or two sections of a course on an A-Day, for example, and then having until the next day to refine and improve their lesson when they teach it again to their remaining one or two sections. And even though students have just four classes per day, with eight blocks over two days, they can still take many courses in one school year.

Why it might not be best for you

Potential challenges of the A/B block schedule include the following:

- **A 90-minute block for intervention or advisory is a lot.** A common approach to the block schedule is for students to take seven classes and to use their eighth block as an intervention or advisory period. The trouble with this approach, as many hundreds of high school educators have shared with us, is that an every-other-day 90-minute block for intervention or advisory is an unhelpfully big chunk of time. Both intervention and advisory are better scheduled as shorter, more focused periods of time. We would recommend schools with block schedules consider scheduling intervention or advisory as a "skinny" 45-minute period.

- **Student absence results in significant missed instruction.** Missing one day of school on the block schedule is like missing two days of school on a traditional schedule. Ouch! For this reason, schools with high rates of absenteeism might think twice about using a block schedule.

- **Adjusting to the block takes effort.** We often hear that teachers who teach in a block schedule love it and cannot imagine teaching shorter periods. Getting to that point, however, takes time and effort. If you switch to a block schedule from a traditional period schedule, be prepared to provide significant training, coaching, and support to teachers to help them use the longer instructional blocks effectively. It can be a two- to three-year process to fully transition curriculum, lesson plans, and instructional practices from a traditional period to a block schedule. (The same is true for teachers moving from a block schedule to a traditional period schedule.)

Avoid the 4×4 semester block schedule

Imagine we are back in the alley where you demanded we answer your question about what is the "best" schedule model. Now you insist we answer the opposite question: what schedule model should you *avoid?* Our answer is the 4×4 semester block schedule, the arrangement in which students take four courses each semester that cover a full year's curriculum. Class periods run the same length as they do in an A/B block schedule, but they are held every day for half the year instead of every other day for the full year.

There are three drawbacks to this model. First, students who take state-tested subjects in the fall are at a disadvantage when testing rolls around in the spring. A student who takes AP Statistics in the fall, for example, must be able to recall material learned in October all the way in May without receiving any instruction or support during the intervening five months. Second, the schedule can prove challenging for foreign language and performing arts classes and for students with learning differences. Taking Spanish 10 during the fall and then potentially not taking Spanish 11 until spring of the following school year (a 12-month gap in instruction) is not the easiest way to learn a new language. And third, the ability to accommodate students who transfer in from schools on a more traditional schedule into a 4×4 semester block schedule is challenging. If a student had been taking seven courses at their previous school, for example, which four do they take first in a 4×4 schedule?

The Rotational Drop Schedule

In this model, students are enrolled in seven courses but only take six courses on any given day, as illustrated in Figure 7.3. Each of the six periods in the day lasts about 55 minutes with approximately two to four minutes for transition between each period. Classes run either the full length of the school year or a semester. Note that it takes seven days for students to rotate through all courses. If the cycle starts on a Monday, for example, the Day 1 schedule would not repeat until the following Wednesday.

When it's a good choice

Consider the rotational drop schedule if your priorities include the following:

- **A high degree of variety.** This model is the opposite of a staid and monotonous schedule, with students attending classes at a different time of day over the course of the week. The variety can keep teachers from feeling like they got the short end of the scheduling stick by always having to teach their toughest section the last period of the day or the period after lunch.

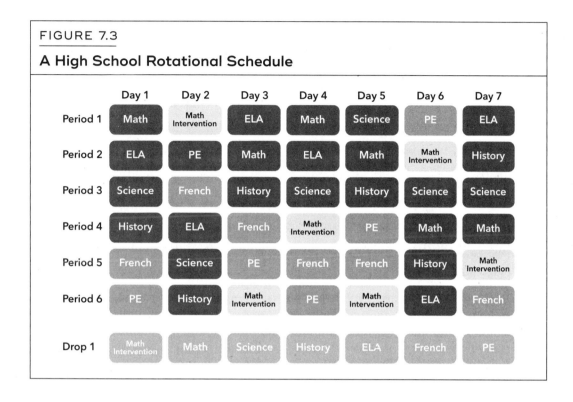

FIGURE 7.3

A High School Rotational Schedule

	Day 1	Day 2	Day 3	Day 4	Day 5	Day 6	Day 7
Period 1	Math	Math Intervention	ELA	Math	Science	PE	ELA
Period 2	ELA	PE	Math	ELA	Math	Math Intervention	History
Period 3	Science	French	History	Science	History	Science	Science
Period 4	History	ELA	French	Math Intervention	PE	Math	Math
Period 5	French	Science	PE	French	French	History	Math Intervention
Period 6	PE	History	Math Intervention	PE	Math Intervention	ELA	French
Drop 1	Math Intervention	Math	Science	History	ELA	French	PE

- **A high number of course offerings.** Students can take seven courses at a time while only actually attending six on any given day. This allows them to engage in a greater variety of courses while not having to manage all seven courses every day.
- **Limiting the impact of late arrival or early dismissal.** The rotational aspect of this model allows schools to reduce the impact of early dismissal, late arrival, field trips, and sports participation. If a student needs to leave early and miss 6th period for their varsity soccer game twice a week, for example, they may miss AP Economics on Monday and Statistics on Thursday, instead of missing AP Economics both days.

Why it might not be best for you

Potential challenges of the rotational drop schedule include the following:

- **"Wait, what day is it?"** A rotational drop schedule is the most confusing schedule for students, teachers, and families to keep track of. It usually does not pass the "wake-up test" we noted above—that is, students and teachers usually must consult a printed schedule or planner to remember what day it is and which classes they have.

- **Incompatibility with external partnerships.** Imagine you work at a local business and want to host high school students for an internship. Now imagine looking at the schedule above and trying to figure out when and how often students would attend the internship. You get the idea: rotational drop schedules can make it very difficult to coordinate outside partnerships, internships, community services, and opportunities at local colleges or universities.

- **Incompatibility with part-time or shared staff.** Rotational drop schedules make it very difficult to effectively use part-time or shared staff. Few are the part-time teachers who are available to teach, say, at 8:30 a.m. on Monday, 2:00 p.m. on Tuesday, and 10:45 a.m. on Thursday.

The Trimester Block Schedule

The trimester block schedule, also known as the 3×5 trimester model, divides the year into three 12-week terms with five approximately 75-minute periods per day. Students take the same classes every day during the term with two to four minutes for transition time between each academic period. Core classes typically run for two trimesters, while electives run either one or three trimesters. Figure 7.4 provides an illustration.

When it's a good choice

Consider the trimester block schedule if your priorities include the following:

- **Long (but not too long) blocks of instruction.** A trimester schedule offers instructional blocks that are longer than a traditional period schedule but shorter than a block schedule. Some teachers consider a 70-minute period the "Goldilocks zone" of period length—enough to get a lot done, but no so long that students run out of steam and lose focus.

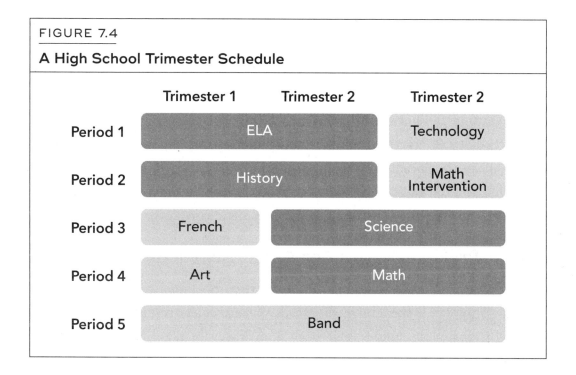

FIGURE 7.4

A High School Trimester Schedule

	Trimester 1	Trimester 2	Trimester 2
Period 1	ELA		Technology
Period 2	History		Math Intervention
Period 3	French	Science	
Period 4	Art	Math	
Period 5	Band		

- **Maximizing course variety.** Students typically can take more courses in a trimester model than any other schedule model (depending on the degree of use of quarter- or semester-long courses in other schedule models). In the example student schedule above, a student would take nine different courses during the school year.

- **Minimizing the number of classes students and teachers have per day.** Like the block schedule, the trimester block schedule is helpful to limit the number of classes and transitions students and teachers have in a given day.

Why it might not be best for you

Potential challenges with the trimester block schedule model include the following:

- **Reduced instructional time per class.** A core course that runs daily for two trimesters with 70-minute periods results in 8,400 minutes of learning time.

This is less than a course taught the full year in a seven-period schedule with 50-minute periods (9,000 minutes learning time). For this reason, the trimester schedule may not work with some schools' local or state course credit hour requirements.

- **Learning gap between trimesters.** Like the 4×4 block schedule, a trimester schedule can create significant gaps in student learning depending on when courses are placed in a student's schedule. For example, a student may take Theater 1 during the first trimester of 10th grade but then not take Theater 2 until the third trimester of 11th grade. That is a gap of over a year.

A Best-Practices Reminder About Instructional Time

Recall the first point we shared in Chapter 2 regarding what research says about schedules: more time spent on quality academic instruction results in more student learning. This finding should weigh heavily on any evaluation of schedule models. Each model has a direct impact on how much time is devoted to each core subject, as tallied in Figure 7.5.

As the figure makes clear, different types of schedule models result in different amounts of instructional time for each course. The seven-period traditional schedule, for example, provides 21 more hours of instructional time per subject than the eight-period schedule, equal to an extra 25 periods of math annually.

◆ ◆ ◆

Is it right to say that a traditional six-period schedule is the "best" because it provides the most instructional time per course? Not necessarily, but if a priority of yours is to offer students the chance to go deep into a small set of courses and subjects, then perhaps it is best for you. On the other hand, if your priority is to offer students a wide variety of course offerings that expose them to many different subjects, then perhaps it's not. What schedule model you choose for your high school ultimately needs to be driven by your priorities and values (see Chapter 2 for more about this).

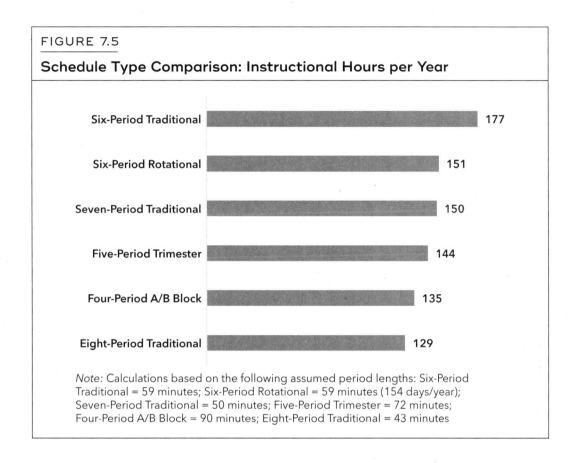

FIGURE 7.5

Schedule Type Comparison: Instructional Hours per Year

Schedule Type	Hours
Six-Period Traditional	177
Six-Period Rotational	151
Seven-Period Traditional	150
Five-Period Trimester	144
Four-Period A/B Block	135
Eight-Period Traditional	129

Note: Calculations based on the following assumed period lengths: Six-Period Traditional = 59 minutes; Six-Period Rotational = 59 minutes (154 days/year); Seven-Period Traditional = 50 minutes; Five-Period Trimester = 72 minutes; Four-Period A/B Block = 90 minutes; Eight-Period Traditional = 43 minutes

For those of you who are thinking, "Wait a second—that's a copout of an answer if I ever heard one," here is the good news: there are elements and components that can (and should!) be incorporated into any of the common high school schedule models we've looked at to make them more strategic and impactful. That's the focus of the next chapter. Read on.

8

Making High School Schedules More Strategic

Ensure your schedule aligns with best practices to supercharge learning and engagement

High school schedules tend to be an order of magnitude more complex and time-consuming to create than middle school or elementary schedules. Scheduling teams at high schools also often spend more time debating schedule design and different schedule models than teams at other grade levels. The irony is that despite the time and attention high schools devote to scheduling, the typical high school schedules we have reviewed lack the key elements of a strategic schedule, none of which are inordinately complex or outrageous to implement. Shifting high school scheduling efforts to focus on five best-practice components can make the whole process easier and improve student outcomes. Those components, which we will detail in this chapter, are as follows:

1. Extra-time intervention provided by content-strong staff.
2. A strategy for authentic relationship building.
3. Ample access to rigor for all.
4. Course work that connects to the "real" world.
5. Time for teacher collaboration.

Our exploration will cover why shifting high school scheduling to focus on these components can boost both student learning outcomes and the connection students feel to content, their teachers, and one another. We will also provide practical advice for adapting your current schedule to include each of these elements rather than designing an entirely new schedule from scratch.

Ensuring Extra-Time Intervention Is Provided by Content-Strong Staff

By 9th grade, core content is complex and builds on nearly a decade of prior learning in school. Even before the pandemic, many students entered high school with skill and content gaps; post-pandemic, the number of students struggling academically has swelled. So it is puzzling to us that many of the high schools we have studied do not incorporate large-scale, best-practice-based intervention practices into the school day.

The research is clear: nearly all students need to learn the current year's grade-level content or they will fall further behind. But as their teachers will quickly point out, they also need to learn skills and content from prior years that they have not yet mastered. It takes one period a day to teach, say, 9th grade math, and it will take another period each day to teach students who struggle with key ideas they have not yet learned from previous math courses. It is simply too much to expect a teacher to teach current content and past content all in one period. Students who are behind academically need extra time to learn.

Who provides this extra instruction matters as much as providing the time itself. There is special skill involved in, say, teaching math to a student who has not quickly grasped math concepts in the past. Often material needs to be presented multiple ways, because simply reteaching a lesson the same way seldom leads to a better outcome. Additionally, every intervention teacher should be able to look at a wrong answer and infer the misunderstanding and unteach the approach that led to it before teaching the new understanding and new approach. All this means that intervention teachers need a deep mastery of the content. Math intervention should be taught by math teachers, literacy intervention by literacy specialists, and so on.

The best way to provide extra-time intervention from content-strong staff at the high school level is through the creation of content-specific intervention courses that are included in the course catalog and built into student and teacher schedules.

Let's look at two high schools that incorporated intervention into their schedule just before the COVID-19 pandemic hit.

At the first high school, the team decided to incorporate a "flex" block at the end of the day. The intention was to give students a 30-minute period each day, during which they could go to teachers for help. If they needed support completing math homework, for example, they would go see the math teacher. The next day if they needed help in science, they could go see the science teacher—or at least this was the idea. In practice, nearly all teachers were assigned to supervise a classroom of 23 to 27 students during the flex block. This made it very difficult for, say, a math teacher supervising a classroom to provide any type of support to students in math, let alone direct instruction tailored to student needs. Eventually, most students ended up staying in the classroom they were assigned when they realized teachers were not in a position to help them. Most students ultimately used the time as a loosely structured study hall.

In contrast, at the second high school, school leadership set up content-specific interventions. They focused on creating a set of math-specific intervention courses for students with a demonstrated need in math fundamentals and a set of literacy-specific intervention courses for students with a demonstrated need for reading support. Students were assigned to the courses based on assessed need, each course had a course code and was incorporated into student schedules, and a teacher with expertise in either math or literacy was assigned to teach the course. A curriculum was set, the teacher provided direct instruction, and students received a grade (pass/fail) and course credit. Students who did not need intervention support took other electives during this block of time.

The experiences of these two high schools highlight the difference between a loosely structured, informally scheduled academic support (e.g., a flex block) and more formally structured and scheduled academic intervention (e.g., a math-specific intervention course). True extra-time academic intervention is targeted, standards-based, curriculum-driven, and taught by a content-strong teacher. Academic support, meanwhile, involves activities like homework help, completing makeup assignments, time on computer programs like iReady, and finishing missed tests. Both have a role but do not expect anything less than best-practice intervention to catch up kids who struggle academically.

Based on lessons learned, we can offer a few pointers for incorporating extra-time intervention into a high school schedule.

Create a course code and make it credit-bearing

Adding a course code and credit to an intervention course helps gives it the necessary "weight" for it to be respected by both students and staff. It makes it clear that it should be taken as seriously as any other course.

Create courses based on the level and type of need

Kids who struggle academically can struggle for different reasons. Often some 9th graders struggle in math because they just did not master 7th and 8th grade concepts, while other students are stuck when it comes to fundamental concepts like number value and fractions. Both groups will benefit from extra-time intervention, but the school should offer two different math intervention courses and assign students based on their need. Similarly, students who struggle to write and those who struggle with reading comprehension or fluency have different needs and benefit from different intervention courses taught by different teachers: one taught by an English teacher and the other by a trained literacy specialist.

Offer intervention as a "skinny" period in block schedules

For schools that run a block schedule, schedule intervention courses as a daily "skinny" period. A 90-minute intervention period every other day, for example, can be very difficult to use as effectively as a 45-minute intervention period every day. Just remember, any "skinny" period needs to dovetail with a second "skinny" period in a student's schedule to fill the full 90-minute block.

Focus on reading, writing, and math

Intervention should focus on equipping students with foundational knowledge and skills in reading, writing, and math. Remember that reading intervention is not the same as writing intervention.

Intervene with one subject at a time

Plenty of students would benefit from intervention in more than one subject. Unfortunately, splitting time across two subjects, like getting math intervention on "even" days and writing intervention on "odd" days, does not provide enough time to catch up in either subject. Students should receive targeted intervention in one subject for an extended period of time (say, for one quarter) and then be reassessed to determine necessary future supports.

Front-load intervention classes

Prioritize intervention during freshman and sophomore years by delaying subjects that do not require four credits for graduation. For example, if only two years of foreign language are needed, delay scheduling Spanish until 10th or 11th grade. If only three years of science are required, enroll students with demonstrated need in a math intervention course when they are in 9th grade, which will help prepare them for the math content of the science courses they will take in grades 10 through 12.

Making Time for Authentic Relationship Building

We noted the importance of building authentic relationships with middle school students in Chapter 6. It is perhaps unsurprising, but strong teacher–student relationships continue to be beneficial as students navigate grades 9 through 12. Many of the same strategies for carving out time for structured relationship building can be applied at the high school level, although the focus and maturity level of conversations should be different.

A 2016 Gallup Education poll found that 29 percent of a nationally representative pool of approximately 730,00 students in grades 5 through 12 were described as "not engaged" (Brenneman, 2016). And this was before the pandemic! Kids who do not care about school will not excel at school. The research is clear that students care more about school when at least one adult at school cares about them. The good news is that, after looking at 1,000 plus high school schedules, we clearly see that high schools are trying to use the schedule to facilitate student and teacher relationships. The bad news is that 29 percent of kids still don't feel engaged, and in some schools the figure is twice this.

Is an advisory period the answer?

The most common example of dedicated relationship-building time in secondary schedules is an advisory period. The fact it is the most common, however, does not mean it is necessarily the most effective.

When we visit schools and ask school leaders to describe their advisory period, it is not uncommon to hear something along the lines of the following: Advisory happens every day for 20 minutes. Advisory classes are 25–30 students, and students are assigned to an advisory at random—typically by homeroom or alphabetically. Advisory teachers are responsible for creating their own activities, which requires the equivalent of another prep. However, this prep is usually at the bottom of their priority list, after lesson planning, grading, and preparing materials for content classes. Students and teachers alike are not entirely clear on the purpose of the advisory time and view advisory more as a study hall than anything else, which results in teachers and staff not assigned to teaching advisory pulling students for academic support during the time.

Done well, advisory periods incorporate consistent rituals and routines and are designed around the needs of students. They provide an opportunity for students and teachers to share their thoughts, discuss timely issues, and develop supportive relationships. They should not be used as a period for announcements, general updates, and homework completion.

Here are two important ways to ensure advisory periods have the impact you intend:

- **Allow students to choose their advisor.** Not every student will click with every teacher. If there has been some negative history between them, there is little chance of students believing that the teacher cares about them (even if they do). Students being able to select the staff member who leads their advisory significantly increases the odds that an authentic relationship will form. Interestingly, when kids get to choose, they often select staff other than teachers, thus increasing the pool and reducing class size. While 100 percent of students may not receive their first choice for advisor, select teachers who are especially popular among students can opt into having a larger advisory (30–40 students) to meet demand. We have also seen advisory structured as an elective; students must request to take advisory and in doing so select the teacher they would like to take advisory with.

- **Provide structured plans for advisors.** Nearly every teacher we meet cares deeply about their students, but this does not mean they all know how to spend 25 minutes building a relationship with a room full of students. Schools should provide a structured plan for how to use the time. Programming should include a mix of activities for relationship building, social-emotional support, and "future planning" (e.g., college or career prep). Support from the school or district should also include providing advisors with training on any program or curriculum used during advisory, adequate prep time to prepare for advisory, and an opportunity to collaborate with other advisors.

Beyond resulting in more engaged students, these two strategies can also make advisory more efficient. We have seen once-a-week best-practice advisory outperform five-days-a-week typical advisory; less time well used for advisory is better than more time poorly planned.

Other relationship-building approaches

Beyond advisory periods, high schools can consider other strategies to facilitate relationship building, such as "clubs" during the school day and lunch with teachers.

Daytime clubs take student choice to the next level. Here is an example: Imagine taking the time formerly allocated to advisory and helping each teacher create a club based on their interest, such as baking, marathoning, board games, or fantasy football. Students opt into a club of their interest. This ensures a common bond with the adult and the other students in the room, both of which can accelerate relationship building.

It is worth noting that relationship building obviously does not *always* require a designated time in the schedule for it to happen. One strategy educators can use that does not require a full period—though still requires a certain degree of fidelity and consistency—is the 2×10 strategy, in which educators select a particular student and set a goal to engage in a two-minute conversation with that student for 10 consecutive school days. Conversations might happen at the beginning or end of a class period, during lunch, or during arrival or dismissal. Research shows that implementing the 2×10 strategy can lead to significant improvements in student behavior, engagement, and the broader classroom climate (Mendler, 2001).

Ensuring Ample Access to Rigor for All

Access to rigorous course work is a key aspect of the equity portion of the strategic scheduling framework.

First, what do we mean by *rigor*? Some think rigor simply means having lots of homework, doing more work, or doing work that's "harder." A better definition focuses on the academic or intellectual challenge of a class and the degree to which the students are prepared, expected, and able to achieve at high levels (Blackburn, 2013). In other words, rigor is less about making things difficult for the sake of being difficult and more about both preparing and asking students to think deeply. A lower-level course can be very rigorous if students are properly prepared *and* required to do the "heavy lifting" when it comes to thinking and engagement with the content. And the awesome thing about rigor is that research shows that when more students are recruited to, prepared for, and supported in rigorous courses in combination with expectations that they do better, they usually *do* perform better (Murray, 2013).

Rigor can help supercharge student learning because it provides an entry point to higher-level content and skills. However, providing equitable access to rigorous courses is a challenge for many high schools. As an example, one study from 2013 determined that, if low-income students and students of color participated in AP and IB at rates similar to their higher-income and white peers, more than half a million students were "missing" from participation in these courses (Theokas & Saaris, 2013). Given findings like this and the data we have seen from high schools across the country, it best to assume access to rigor is inequitable until proven otherwise. To assess whether all students have equitable access to rigorous courses, schools need to ask three important questions.

How many students are taking rigorous courses?

Start by examining what advanced and high-rigor courses students are taking. One STEM-focused high school we worked with begin this process by looking at the enrollment in each level in the math and science departments. Being a STEM-oriented school, the school leaders went in confident that their high-rigor courses were packed to the gills. But when they tallied enrollment by course level, they were surprised at what they saw:

Math Enrollment by Course Level
15% of students in AP courses
21% of students in honors courses
49% of students in general-level courses
15% of students in below-grade-level courses

Science Enrollment by Course Level
4% of students in AP courses
10% of students in honors courses
84% percent of students in general-level courses
2% of students in below-grade-level courses

School leadership found that the math department offered many AP and honors courses, which aligned with the school's overall STEM mission, but also many remediation-level courses teaching below grade level that did not appear to set students up for success in future math classes. In this STEM-focused school, fully one in six students was not enrolled in a grade-level math class. This was a surprise, but it would have been easily discovered had anyone looked.

The leadership team was also surprised to find that the science department had far fewer students enrolled in honors and advanced-level courses than the math department; they had assumed if the math department had many students in advanced courses, then the science department would have a similar number, especially given the school's STEM focus. It was not the case.

This school's experience highlights an important reality. After studying many hundreds of schools, we know that a wide variation in access to rigor by department is the norm, not the exception. It turns out that department leader preference and department practices, not student ability, explain much of the difference. Some departments require a teacher recommendation to enroll in honors or AP courses, and others do not. Some departments have a minimum grade point average for entrance, and some do not. Some counsel all but the most able students to avoid high-rigor classes. In a world just starting to come to grips with the many forms of bias, leaving entrance criteria to each department seems a recipe for inequity. Ideally, all students who can master the most rigorous courses should be encouraged to enroll and given the support they need to succeed.

Which students take rigorous courses?

Once the high school knew what enrollment each level of course had, they then begin to examine student enrollment patterns, which provide an additional metric to determine the status of access to rigor. They collected enrollment figures for all honors and advanced courses in math and science and disaggregated the data by student group, as show in Figure 8.1.

The school leadership team quickly saw that some student demographic groups (Asian, white) were enrolled in honors and advanced courses at a disproportionate rate relative to their peers. This is the case in many high schools. In fact, while the College Board has reported that overall AP enrollment for all student demographic groups has steadily grown over time—in the decade between 2001 and 2011, for

FIGURE 8.1

Honors/Advanced Course Enrollment by Demographic Group

Student Demographic Group	Percent of Total District Enrollment	Percent of Total Honors and Advanced Course Enrollment
Asian or Pacific Islander	22%	38%
Black	14%	8%
Latinx	35%	17%
Native American	3%	2%
White	26%	35%
Total	**100%**	**100%**

example, the number of high school graduates who took at least one AP exam increased by 95 percent—program expansion has *not* addressed the gap in participation by race, ethnicity, or socioeconomic status (Theokas & Saaris, 2013).

To help figure out why enrollment in advanced and honors courses varied so significantly between student groups, the leadership team at the STEM high school investigated course placement and prerequisite policies. They saw an overreliance on teacher recommendations—which, despite teachers' best intentions, can be biased—and course grades, which can be a better measure of student effort than actual mastery of content or skills. Teachers saw prerequisites as immovable, which prevented otherwise capable students from joining courses, and students who traditionally did not take advanced courses were rarely recruited or encouraged to join. All of this contributed to underenrollment in advanced courses on the part of Black and Latinx students.

Which students succeed in rigorous courses?

The final question the high school leadership team examined to assess access to rigor was how well students who take high-rigor courses do in those courses.

They reviewed the pass rate of students taking AP courses in the math and science departments and compared their pass rates to national data (see Figure 8.2).

Looking at the numbers, the leadership team saw that the achievement of students in AP math courses was far below the achievement of students in AP science courses. To figure out why, the team first looked back at the original data they had compiled to determine what courses were offered in each department. Remember how they noticed that 15 percent of total math department enrollment was in below grade-level courses? Turns out these courses were not preparing students well for eventual enrollment in advanced courses. Students were missing key skills, and their grades in the lower-level courses were not valid indicators of their overall preparedness. The lowest-level math courses were also taught by the least experienced, least effective teachers in the department. (The science department, to its credit, had its more effective, most experienced teachers teach at least one section of a lower-level science course.) So, the school offered plenty of advanced math courses but did not build up student skills over time in a way that prepared them to succeed in those courses. Remember: rigor means asking more of students *and* preparing them to meet those expectations.

FIGURE 8.2

Comparison Data on the Pass Rates for the AP Math and Science Tests

Department	Course	% Passed (Score of 3-5)	National Pass Rate*	Difference from National Pass Rate
Math	AP Calculus AB	21%	56%	−35%
	AP Calculus BC	17%	77%	−60%
	AP Statistics	33%	60%	−27%
Science	AP Biology	96%	68%	+28%
	AP Chemistry	94%	54%	+40%

Source: The College Board, 2022.

Reviewing the number of students taking AP science math and sciences courses (see Figure 8.3), the leadership team noticed something else. While the students who did take AP science courses did extremely well on AP science tests, just 20 students took AP science courses—a quarter of the number of students who were enrolled in AP math courses. The school realized that there was an opportunity to expand the number of students who took AP science courses given the effectiveness of the existing curriculum and teachers in the science department, as well as an opportunity to reexamine the math curriculum, coaching of math teachers, and enrollment in AP math courses, given students' comparatively low pass rates on AP math tests.

Finally, be very careful not to confuse the *appearance* of rigor with *actual* access to rigor for all. Some high schools become committed to enrolling many students into high-rigor classes, which is good, but then choose to ignore the achievement of students in those classes. Interestingly, these schools are often extremely proud of their "accomplishment" just the same.

Here are two pieces of advice to help you avoid this hollow victory. First, never eliminate lower-level courses without adding best-practice extra-time intervention with content-strong teachers. Again, a course that students are not prepared

---

FIGURE 8.3

Enrollment in AP Math and Sciences Courses and National Pass Rate Comparison

Department	Course	# of Students Enrolled	% Passed (Score of 3-5)	Difference from National Pass Rate
Math	AP Calculus AB	25	21%	−40%
	AP Calculus BC	26	17%	−60%
	AP Statistics	27	33%	−27%
Science	AP Biology	11	96%	+28%
	AP Chemistry	9	94%	+40%

for skill-wise is not rigorous; it is problematic, even damaging, for the kids, and it is frustrating for their teachers. Lower-level courses should be removed from the course catalog only if extra-help intervention classes are added at the same time and the students who would have been enrolled in the lower-level courses are enrolled in both the higher-level course *and* extra-time intervention.

Similarly, enrolling students in AP, IB, and honors courses is not the same as students mastering this challenging content. Some schools have doubled, even tripled, enrollment in AP classes (while also increasing academic supports available to students in AP-tested subjects) and seen AP test pass rates hold steady. This is a success story. Other schools fly the "mission accomplished" banner just for increasing enrollment. One high school was proud to report that 100 percent of its seniors took AP Calculus or AP Statistics. Seems impressive until you see that only 5 percent of those seniors got a passing score on the AP exam. This is not what success looks like.

Providing a Connection to the "Real World"

Nate likes math. He always has. Throughout high school, he likely solved 10,000 equations for x. Whether it was the angle of a polygon, the speed of a train, or the intersection of two lines, he was assigned a lot of math problems, and most of them ended with figuring out what x equaled. He was always more than happy to do so.

When Nate interviews students today, he often hears, "What I learn in school doesn't matter to me. Why do I care what x equals?" That is a fair question, and it's being asked more often by more students. In the same way that the COVID-19 pandemic prompted a lot of adults to question the meaning of their work, more students seem to be wondering what the point of their schoolwork is and if *any* of the classes on their schedule truly matter in the long run.

A strategic high school schedule can provide connections to the "real" world and help students see the relevance of their course work and reinvest in it. For schedule makers, the levers to adjust fall into the course offerings section of the strategic scheduling framework.

The easiest way to ensure your course offerings resonate with students is simply to ask them what courses they think would be relevant to their future. Surveying students about classes they wish were offered can help school leaders revise elective offerings. This is how one school learned that students wanted courses on social justice themes and another school, with many students from Southeast Asia, learned that classes on both the history and literature of the region would feel relevant.

Then there is the growing trend of concretely connecting kids to the real world through internships, work study, and dual enrollment at local colleges. This is a good start. The next step is to bring these ideas to scale. One high school we worked with was proud of its internship and early college (dual credit) program. Staff beamed as they explained all the possibilities—the options it provided for students interested in nursing, engineering, marketing, law, and criminal justice to take college courses, earn college credits, and start pursuing career interests. Unfortunately, only 20 students from this large high school took part. A great program would engage 10 or 20 times more students.

What that school might have done to increase program participation was bring the college course work to students rather than asking students to take themselves to the college course work. That's what a district in Colorado did by arranging for college faculty to teach regular college courses inside a high school building. The rooms, professors, and enrolled students were all included in the high school schedule, just like any other course.

Another trend we hope to see more of is connecting students to "real-world" futures that do not necessarily include college. High-quality career technical education (CTE) can engage large numbers of unengaged students and set them on the path to a great job, income, and life. A student who learns a trade like plumbing or carpentry can easily out-earn many college graduates, and they often greatly enjoy their work. Of the CTE students we meet, the most engaged ones feel that they are mastering a valuable trade skill and are acutely aware that they will graduate with robust job prospects. While most high schools have expanded their career pathways and CTE offerings, many are not tightly connected to the real world, and students know this.

One high school we worked with created a number of career pathways, including one called Allied Health that was intended to energize students who wanted to become nurses and other healthcare providers. It was a great idea, but the execution was lacking. It called for students to take a single course on the topic over four years, meet with a nurse for a few hours, and take a field trip to a hospital. That is not enough to generate four years of high school engagement.

In many other schools, even the more traditional CTE programs seem to be moving away from building marketable skills and toward general career awareness. They expose kids to many possible careers or give them an opportunity to learn a bit about a field. One school required students to take a career survey course but did not offer in-depth options in each field. Another school taught automotive maintenance, but the course focused exclusively on simple tasks, like changing spark plugs and oil, even though there was a full auto repair shop across the street from the school. Some of the most engaged students we meet feel they are mastering a valuable trade skill and are acutely aware that they will graduate with robust job prospects.

One way to signal to students that what they are learning is valued by the real world is to link completion of course work to earning an industry-validated certification. The other way to message their CTE classes matter is to build internships with large employers who will hire the students over the summer and upon graduation.

Providing Time for Teacher Collaboration

Research confirms that quality collaboration leads to better teaching (Schleifer et al., 2017). The positive effects of well-used teacher collaboration time include improved self-efficacy, increased teaching effectiveness, and higher-quality instruction (Reeves et al., 2017).

There are two important types of collaboration to consider when scheduling: *content planning* and *grade-level/schoolwide planning*.

Content planning collaboration includes

- Reviewing curriculum, unit pacing, and lesson planning.
- Analyzing and discussing assessment results.

- Learning, sharing, and improving instructional strategies for teaching specific content or lessons.

Grade-level/school planning collaboration includes

- Discussing student social, emotional, and other nonacademic needs.
- Aligning behavioral expectations and cultural norms.
- Preparing events and school climate–building activities.

So, if collaboration time is definitively helpful, what's the catch? There are two catches, actually: finding time in the schedule for it to happen and making sure that the time is well used.

How to find time for collaboration

"I have never had so much time to plan and collaborate with my peers. It has been incredibly helpful!" This was a common refrain we heard from educators during the early months of the pandemic. Throughout spring 2020, it seemed like most of the schools and districts we worked with had set up blocks of virtual planning and collaboration time for teachers. The kind of content and curriculum planning sessions that used to happen only once or twice per year were happening once or twice each week via Zoom. Many districts even aligned planning blocks across multiple schools to allow, say, all middle school science teachers to collaborate virtually on lesson planning on a regular basis. Talk about an unexpected, positive change driven by a challenging situation!

Despite the positive reception of these virtual planning bocks, many schools and districts have since moved away from them, as they required a significant reduction in instructional time. But the more innovative schools and districts we partner with have continued to thoughtfully carve out time (virtually and in-person) for teacher planning and collaboration. Here are some of the specific methods they use that you might try.

- **Use scheduling software to find common planning time.** If a school priority is to ensure all 9th grade math teachers have common content planning time daily, for example, use the prioritization features included in your scheduling software to make it happen. An expert scheduler can harness the power of programs like PowerSchool or Infinite Campus to create common prep periods for selected groups of teachers.

- **Incorporate regular early-dismissal or late-arrival days.** How do you find time in the schedule to facilitate grade-level collaboration, content-specific collaboration, cross-team collaboration, *and* cross-school collaboration? Simple: create a schedule that includes regular early dismissal for students. Finding time for different teams and combinations of teachers and staff to meet at the same school, let alone between schools, is challenging in any schedule. The only "easy button" solution to this challenge is to create regularly scheduled days in which students leave early (or arrive late) and allow teachers a few hours to collaborate. We know it seems hard to reduce students' time with teachers, but 160 hours of a well-planned course can be more impactful than 180 hours without the benefit of truly flexible planning time.

- **Schedule "internal" early-release days.** This is a similar idea to the one above, but with a twist. Instead of dismissing students from school early, consider an "internal" early-release day: students do not attend regular classes but do not go home either. Instead, they participate in specially scheduled in-school activities—a field day hosted by noncore teachers, enrichment activities run by external partners like the YMCA, grade-level SEL-related sessions facilitated by school administration and guidance staff, and so on. Core content teachers use the afternoon to meet and plan, either virtually or in person.

- **Align bell schedules and planning periods.** A district with five high schools made a point to implement a common bell schedule across campuses and align the planning periods of content teachers to allow for regular virtual cross-campus planning time. For example, all 9th grade English teachers in the district now have planning time at the same time every day and join a biweekly virtual collaboration session hosted by the district's English lead.

It turns out there are many ways to find the time in the schedule for common planning, but it will only happen if you make it a top priority.

How to ensure planning time is well used

Of course, setting aside time for planning and collaboration does not mean that teachers will know how or be prepared to use that time effectively. Planning time needs an agenda, a focus, and an expert.

Having clarity on the purpose of each session—lesson planning, reviewing data, discussing individual students, and so on—is Step 1. Each session should have a very narrow focus so that each teacher leaves it knowing which concrete action they will take next. Next, every session needs someone with related expertise to guide the team's work and ensure they keep to the session's stated purpose. This can be a highly effective teacher, a department chair, or an instructional coach.

We can point to a school that went all in on teacher planning time in a way that serves as a caution rather than an inspiration. Although they reserved the time and met regularly, they failed to use their time strategically. Without an agenda, few agreed upon each session's goals, and with no clear leader, the conversation was dominated by a few veteran teachers jumping from topic to topic as they pleased.

◆ ◆ ◆

The next step toward developing a strategic high school schedule is to complete the self-assessment in Appendix C (see p. 203). It will help you take stock of your current schedule and identify how well it is set up to align with the best practices we have highlighted.

In the next chapter, we will examine the importance of staffing precisely to match enrollment and share strategies for how you can create more opportunities for students without adding new staff.

9

Precision Staffing

*Staff precisely to course enrollment to free up
funds for other priorities*

Staff shortages are a long-standing challenge for many schools. Between 2009 and 2014, the most recent years for which data is available, enrollment in teacher education programs dropped from 691,000 to 451,000, a 35 percent reduction (Sutcher et al., 2016). The problem of fewer entering the profession is compounded by the number who are leaving. When the National Education Association surveyed nearly 2,700 teachers in June 2021, 32 percent responded that they intended to leave teaching earlier than they had originally planned (Rodriguez-Delgado et al., 2021). Finding personnel to fill an increasing number of open teaching positions is expected to be even more challenging with the end of Elementary and Secondary School Emergency Relief (ESSER) funding.

Now, some good news: strategic scheduling and staffing can help to address both challenges.

At its core, staffing precisely to course enrollment is about maximizing the reach and impact of every teacher by freeing up staff to teach more sections of electives, intervention, or other courses. Simply put, schools can offer their students more without having to hire additional staff *or* overloading the staff they have. We have seen schools that have embraced this approach save $200,000–$300,000 per school—not an insignificant amount to reroute to other priorities and programming. This is a critical point: precise and efficient staffing is not efficiency for efficiency's sake; it's a tool in service of student learning, opportunity, and choice.

Although staffing to enrollment is beneficial at all grade levels, it's especially so in high schools, which typically have the largest student enrollments, the highest staff counts, and the most courses offered. Making scheduling and staffing more precise at the high school level therefore often represents the biggest opportunity for most districts. With that in mind, this chapter will outline the methodologies and strategies high schools (and many middle schools, for that matter) can use to staff more precisely and provide a greater variety of academic, intervention, and enrichment course offerings to students at no added cost.

Why You Shouldn't Skip This Chapter

Perhaps you are thinking, *We already staff very precisely. We spend hours, weeks even, on our staffing plan. Maybe I can skip this chapter.* About 95 percent of the schools we mentioned—the ones that that freed up $200,000 or more—initially thought this too. A good many were absolutely certain they were staffed as precisely as possible. And it is true that they did staff thoughtfully, just not to the decimal place. They rounded up, made a few simplifying assumptions, and trusted their scheduling software too much. You too might be surprised at how big an opportunity there is at your school to do more with the same FTE (full-time employees).

One high school we partnered with in Connecticut provides a great example. A quick review of the school's course and staffing data revealed there was significant variation in class sizes within in the math department, with some sections enrolling just 11 students while other sections of the same subject had 32 students. This variation in class sizes was representative of what we found in the school's other departments as well.

Variation in class size is not necessarily a negative thing; it makes sense for some classes, such as a math intervention course, to have lower enrollment than, say, an honors geometry course. Here is the kicker, though: unintentional variation can be a symptom of larger issues. In the case of this Connecticut high school, there were a number of reasons behind the variation in class size:

- Staffing at the high school rolled over year after year with very little change even though the school's enrollment had decreased by 5 percent over the past 10 years.
- Courses were added over the years, but very few were removed. Some of this was driven by basic human psychology: it is fun to add, but painful to take away.
- There was a course minimum enrollment of 15 students, but it was not enforced consistently. Very few teachers knew the cutoff existed, and there was no clear protocol for who would ultimately decide whether a course should be added or removed.
- In an effort to honor students' first-choice course selections, some classes just "had to be much smaller" than others.
- Every teacher had a full schedule, so the schedule looked like it was efficient.
- The school's scheduler said there were no alternatives—the current schedule was the best that could be done.

Few in the district were aware of the implications from their current approach to staffing, which included the following:

- **A limit on the number of academic intervention courses the school could provide.** They tacitly devoted extra staffing to new, relatively small courses that often served high-achieving students instead of additional intervention or acceleration courses that could support students who were struggling.
- **A high number of low-enrollment courses and single-section courses.** The single-section courses were often prioritized during the scheduling process and "clogged up" the schedule. This resulted in fewer students receiving courses they ranked high during the course selection process.
- **Students missing out on the electives they wanted.** Some students were scheduled into unpopular electives, while some of the most in-demand classes were oversubscribed, meaning some students were locked out from taking them.

The school learned that by staffing more precisely in just the math department, it could free up 1.2 FTE—the equivalent of six sections of extra-time math intervention. Staffing more precisely across *all* the departments could free up 4.4 FTE—or a total of 22 sections! This represented $330,000 in potential funds for reinvestment, all without reducing course offerings or increasing class size beyond existing district targets. That is the power of strategic scheduling and staffing! Keep reading to learn the strategies this high school used to make this happen.

An Overview of the Precision Staffing Process

Staffing precisely to course enrollment is surprisingly straightforward, although it does take careful planning, strong data systems, proactive management of tradeoffs, and an expert scheduler. In our experience, the work is best tackled in three phases:

1. **Understand what you have.** Get an accurate count of current enrollment, the number of sections offered for each course, and FTE by department and course.

2. **Calculate what you will need.** Using next year's enrollment projections by course, calculate the required number of sections and FTE by department for next year's schedule.

3. **Adjust for actual enrollment.** Adjust section counts over the summer and the first weeks of school based on actual enrollment numbers.

We will walk you through each of these phases, providing guidance and illustrations to clarify how you might bring this staffing approach to the school you lead.

Phase 1: Understanding What You Have

You need an accurate count of your current enrollment, the number of course sections, and FTE by department and course. Without this kind of detailed knowledge of how your school is currently staffed, you cannot know where there is opportunity to improve or identify areas of need. For example:

• Do all teachers have full workloads? If not, how does this vary by grade level or department?

- Which departments have staffing capacity to offer more intervention and elective offerings, and by how many FTE?
- How does average class size vary by course type (core, noncore), course level (general, honors, AP, etc.), and department (math, science, etc.)?
- Are existing class-size guidelines reflected in the schedule? If not, how can you address the deviation without reducing offerings?

Analyze class size by individual course

To begin to build foundational understanding of current classes, first pull current enrollment for each section of each course from your scheduling or student information system. From there, you can quickly calculate average class size by dividing course enrollment by section count to determine variation in average class size across courses. We will use a math department as an example (see Figure 9.1).

As you can see, the average class size varies across courses, from 18 to 28 students. The average class size of higher-level math courses (Geometry, Pre-Calculus, Calculus) is higher than lower-level math courses (Algebra, Honors Algebra), and, interestingly, the average class size of Honors Algebra is lower than that of regular Algebra.

Let's now look at a noncore department—in this case, the visual arts department (see Figure 9.2).

FIGURE 9.1

Average Class Sizes in the Math Department

Math Course Offerings	Course Enrollment	Section Count	Average Class Size
Algebra	310	14	22
Honors Algebra	90	5	18
Geometry	240	10	24
Pre-Calculus	220	8	27
Calculus	112	4	28

FIGURE 9.2

Average Class Sizes in the Visual Arts Department

Visual Arts Course Offerings	Course Enrollment	Section Count	Average Class Size
Animation	78	3	26
Ceramics & Sculpture I	13	1	13
Drawing I	80	5	16
Painting I	54	3	18
Painting II	34	2	17

Here we see that outside of animation, average class sizes in visual arts are significantly smaller those in the math department. This is representative of what we commonly see in many high schools: core classes (e.g., math, science, English, social studies) are often larger, on average, than noncore classes (e.g., visual arts, performing arts, technology).

Examine the range of class sizes

Average class size is not enough to understand the full picture of current course and staffing practices. You also need to look at the range of class sizes in each course, as shown in Figure 9.3.

With the class-size range tabulated, a few other things become clear. Advanced courses in math, such as Honors Algebra and Calculus, have a wider range in class size than general-level courses. Visual arts classes have a wider class-size range than math classes in general, which speaks to the number of very low-enrollment sections in the visual arts department.

Gaining clarity on existing enrollment can help you build a nuanced understanding of where there are potential opportunities to staff more precisely for the next school year. Remember: the purpose of this exercise is not to find what is "wrong" with the schedule but rather to identify opportunities where you can provide more

FIGURE 9.3

Average Class-Size Ranges

Department	Course Offering	Course Enrollment	Section Count	Average Class Size	Class-Size Range
Math	Algebra	310	14	22	21–23
	Honors Algebra	90	5	18	13–23
	Geometry	240	10	24	22–26
	Pre-Calculus	220	8	27	26–28
	Calculus	112	4	22	18–26
Visual Arts	Animation	78	3	26	24–28
	Ceramics & Sculpture I	13	1	13	13
	Drawing I	80	5	16	12–20
	Painting I	54	3	18	16–20
	Painting II	34	2	17	10–24

learning opportunities to students, like additional electives or intervention courses, at no additional cost and within existing class-size targets. In the example above, it appears there is opportunity to staff more precisely in Honors Algebra, Calculus, and most of the visual arts classes. Keep reading to see how this plays out.

Phase 2: Calculating What You Will Need

With a solid sense of what you have, you can start to figure out how to make your staffing more precise.

Use next year's course enrollment in your calculations

Instead of using *current* course enrollment data, work with next year's enrollment projections, like what is shown in Figure 9.4. In this example, enrollment projections appear relatively similar to the previous year's figures.

FIGURE 9.4

Projected Course Enrollments

Department	Course Name	Projected Course Enrollment
Math	Algebra	330
	Honors Algebra	95
	Geometry	250
	Pre-Calculus	235
	Calculus	85
Visual Arts	Animation	88
	Ceramics & Sculpture I	17
	Drawing I	75
	Painting I	55
	Painting II	30

Factor in class-size targets and the maximum allowable class sizes

Many districts set different targets for core and noncore classes and class level as well. To keep our example simple, we will assume math courses have a target class size of 25 students and a maximum size of 28 students, while visual arts classes have a target class size of 27 students and a maximum of 30 students. Figure 9.5 summarizes the class-size criteria. In practice, the target and maximum class size might differ by course.

Notice that the school in this example wisely set different class-size targets for the different departments. This is not always the case. We have found that it is more common for schools to set universal class-size targets regardless of grade level, department, or level of rigor. Differentiating class-size targets, however, is an important tool in any strategic scheduler's toolkit and is one way a school can align its course and staffing practices with its priorities.

FIGURE 9.5

Targeted and Maximum Class Sizes

Department	Course Name	Projected Course Enrollment	Target Class Size	Maximize Class Size
Math	Algebra	330	25	28
	Honors Algebra	95	25	28
	Geometry	250	25	28
	Pre-Calculus	235	25	28
	Calculus	85	25	28
Visual Arts	Animation	88	27	30
	Ceramics & Sculpture I	17	27	30
	Drawing I	75	27	30
	Painting I	55	27	30
	Painting II	30	27	30

Calculate the number of sections needed for each course

Using the class-size targets and maximums, it's possible to calculate the number of sections required for each course by simply dividing the projected enrollment by target class size. For example, 330 students taking Algebra with a target of 25 students equals 13.2 sections. It is fine to round this down to 13 because the resulting average class size (25.4) is below the maximum allowed for math courses (28). In reality, most sections of Algebra will have 25 students, and a few will have one or two additional students. Figure 9.6 provides a summary of these results.

Identify FTE requirements

Finally, with section counts calculated, determine the required FTE for each course and department by dividing the section count by the full teaching load of a teacher. In our example (see Figure 9.7), each full-time teacher teaches five sections.

FIGURE 9.6

Projected Section Counts

Department	Course Name	Projected Course Enrollment	Target Class Size	Maximum Class Size	Projected Section Count
Math	Algebra	330	25	28	13
	Honors Algebra	95	25	28	4
	Geometry	250	25	28	10
	Pre-Calculus	235	25	28	9
	Calculus	85	25	28	3
Visual Arts	Animation	88	27	30	3
	Ceramics & Sculpture I	17	27	30	1
	Drawing I	75	27	30	3
	Painting I	55	27	30	2
	Painting II	30	27	30	1

FIGURE 9.7

Projected Full–Time Employee (FTE) Requirements

Department	Course Name	Projected Section Count	Projected FTE Needed
Math	Algebra	13	2.6
	Honors Algebra	4	0.8
	Geometry	10	2.0
	Pre-Calculus	9	1.8
	Calculus	3	0.6
	TOTAL	—	**7.8**
Visual Arts	Animation	3	0.6
	Ceramics & Sculpture I	1	0.2
	Drawing I	3	0.6
	Painting I	2	0.4
	Painting II	1	0.2
	TOTAL	—	**2.0**

With current and projected enrollment, staffing, FTE, and average class-size data calculated, you can see what a difference more precise staffing makes (see Figure 9.8).

It is clear school leaders made a few decisions to staff more precisely for the next school year based on projected course enrollment. To begin with, despite an anticipated increase in total enrollment, one section of Algebra was dropped to bring the average class size closer to the target class size of 25 students. One section of Honors Algebra was also removed for the same reason, though in this case, the school is still in a tricky spot—the projected average class size is still four students below the target class size, but removing a second section would result in a projected average class size of 32 students, which is above the district's class-size maximum of 30 students. A section of Calculus was also removed, resulting in a projected average class size of 30 students—above the target class size but still acceptable to school leaders and

FIGURE 9.8

Full-Time Employee (FTE) Savings Realized

Department	Course Name	Current FTE	Projected FTE	FTE Change
Math	Algebra	2.8	2.6	−0.2
	Honors Algebra	1	0.8	−0.2
	Geometry	2	2	0
	Pre-Calculus	1.6	1.8	0.2
	Calculus	0.8	0.6	−0.2
	TOTAL	—	—	**−0.4**
Visual Arts	Animation	0.6	0.6	0
	Ceramics & Sculpture I	0.2	0.2	0
	Drawing I	1	0.6	−0.4
	Painting I	0.6	0.4	−0.2
	Painting II	0.4	0.2	−0.2
	TOTAL	—	—	**−0.8**

the math department. One section of Pre-Calculus was added to account for an increase in projected enrollment.

Overall, the change of removing three sections and adding one section resulted in a net reduction of 0.4 in FTE. This allowed the math department to add two new sections of math-specific intervention.

In the visual arts department, the number of sections of Drawing I, Painting I, and Painting II were all reduced to staff more precisely to class-size targets. This also reduced the range in class sizes. The removal of the four sections resulted in a net reduction of 0.8 in FTE and allowed the visual arts department to add a new set of courses in photography the following year, all of which could be taught by existing staff members.

In total across the two departments, staffing more precisely freed up approximately $100,000 and allowed the school to offer two new sections of intervention and four new sections of electives. Now imagine the combined impact of this approach to staffing across *all departments* in the school and you can really see the value and importance of staffing precisely!

Phase 3: Adjusting for Actual Enrollment

If a school stopped after completing Phase 2, it would definitely have more precise staffing than most schools we have worked with. But some districts take precision staffing to an even higher level. They adjust staffing and scheduling once again after they know the actual course enrollments, taking into account changes over the summer and even drop/add course changes during the first week of school. At this point, some veteran schedulers might be saying, "That is all well and good, but I have never *ever* been part of a scheduling process when projected enrollment aligned exactly to *actual* enrollment." In the scheduling trainings we facilitate, many a school scheduler has shared how frustrating it is to have to adjust course enrollments and section counts over the summer to keep up with fluctuating student enrollment numbers.

It is undoubtedly a hassle to have to revise carefully crafted schedules over the summer and again in the first few weeks of school, but it is good scheduling practice—and the most precise way to match staffing to actual enrollment. One large district reran their high school schedules a week before school started and then checked staffing requirements the week after school began. Then they issued revised schedules 10 days after school started, added intervention sections if staff were freed up, opted to leave a few last-minute vacancies unfilled, and even shifted staff between schools as needed. We know this seems like a lot of work and disruption, but it seemed normal in the district and reduced overall staffing by about three percent a year, which is $350,000 in a 2,000-student high school.

Although this kind of staffing and scheduling adjustment may sound difficult, even crazy, it does not have to be. There are a number of strategies schools and schedulers can use to make the work easier.

Proactively manage course-change requests

Set and communicate a firm deadline to teachers, counselors, students, and families by which date course requests must be finalized. Share that if students request a change over the summer, there is no guarantee the change can be honored.

Hand out *provisional* schedules in the spring

Though sharing actual schedules with teachers and students in May or June can help put everyone at ease before heading into the summer, schools that take this approach report often find subsequent changes to the schedule frustrating and anxiety provoking. They worked so hard, and for what? When sharing provisional schedules with students, reveal only the name of the courses they are expected to be enrolled in—not which section you have slotted them into (for multi-section courses) or what periods in the day those courses will occupy. Being nonspecific in this way helps avoid scenarios like students requesting to be transferred to a different section of a course so they can be with their friends. This advice holds when sharing teachers' provisional schedules. Tell them the courses they will be teaching and how many sections of each, but not the exact periods.

Require students to select alternative or multiple preferences

Requiring students to share preferences for more courses than they will actually take during the course selection process provides a scheduler with greater flexibility and decreases the odds of disappointing students by giving them little or nothing on their list.

Allow students to cast forward course requests

At the high school level, approach course selection with students as a multi-year planning process instead of a semester-to-semester or year-to-year process. Allow counselors to partner with students during their freshman year and build a "high school course pathway" that outlines the courses a student plans to take throughout their high school career. Not only will this help you more accurately project staffing needs multiple years out, but it will also help students by giving them a big-picture sense of what they will be building toward.

Watch Out for Default Settings on Scheduling Software

Most high schools use scheduling software such as PowerSchool, Aspen, or a scheduling module that has been built into the district's student information system (SIS). These programs are incredibly powerful, but be careful how you use them.

The software is usually designed to set up every teacher in the school with a full teaching load, based on student course requests. The program asks how many science teachers you have—but it does not let you know how many you will actually *need*. It assumes you have the right number of teachers. For example, if 300 students are taking math and three math teachers are available, the scheduling software will create a full schedule for each math teacher—in this case, every teacher will be set up to teach five sections of 20 students each. An expert scheduler knows to watch out for this and adjust the settings in the software so that, for example, two of these math teachers will have five sections of 25 students each, and the third teacher will have three sections of 25 students. Making this adjustment frees the third teacher to teach three new sections of math intervention free of charge.

We'll talk more in Chapter 11 about the importance of utilizing scheduling expertise when designing and building schedules.

With a course plan mapped out, students are generally less inclined to make abrupt or last-minute course selection changes. This multi-year course information is loaded into the scheduling and course management software and can be adjusted (if necessary) as students progress through high school.

The Special Challenge of Low-Enrollment and Single-Section Courses

Even with precise staffing, low-enrollment and single-section courses can complicate your search for efficiency. The threshold for what constitutes a low-enrollment course varies by district, though a reasonable benchmark to use is any course with 15 or fewer students.

Low-enrollment courses may be offered for a number of reasons: strong interest from a small number of students, teacher desire to teach the course, or inertia when a course that was full in a previous year ends up under-enrolled. Comments we commonly hear from educators about low-enrollment courses include the following:

- "We pride ourselves on meeting the needs and interests of all students. Having a bunch of low-enrollment courses is the price we happily pay to provide a broad selection."
- "We have shifted from a student choice model to letting the teachers teach their personal favorites rather than letting student interest dictate the courses offered."
- "I would hate to not offer many of these courses."
- "There are very few new course proposals that are turned down and very few courses that are removed or deleted from the block. Some of this is because of staff culture (we're pretty nonconfrontational), and some of this is because it is not really clear what the standards to 'accept' or 'reject' a new course are."

It is not uncommon for us to find a school in which teachers, students, and families happily accept low-enrollment classes, while principals and district administrators are frustrated by the prevalence of the very same low-enrollment courses.

Fortunately, there are strategies to reduce very small classes, keep all the choices offered to students, and balance the preferences of all stakeholders.

Alternate when the course is offered

Reduce the frequency of when the low-enrollment courses are offered to every other year or every other semester. This might mean offering a low-enrollment advanced course (e.g., AP European History) every other year or creative writing every other semester. Offering a course less frequently often doubles the number of students in the class when it *is* offered.

Combine low-enrollment courses with related courses

Get class enrollment closer to the guidelines. For example, combine a section of Spanish 3 with 14 students with a section of Spanish 4 with 9 students or watercolors with AP Art and Art 4. This is most common in noncore offerings like art, where students work mostly independently, or high-level world language classes.

Set minimum enrollment thresholds

Only offer a course if a minimum enrollment threshold is met. In many schools and districts we work with, this threshold is around 15 students. For the threshold to be effective, three things must happen:

1. School leaderships, teachers, students, and families must be aware of the threshold. Be sure to note the threshold in the course catalog and course selection guidance, and note that the courses listed in the course catalog may not run if they do not meet minimum enrollment.
2. A clear process and ultimate decision maker must exist to determine exceptions. This is usually the principal in large districts or an assistant superintendent of teaching and instruction in smaller districts.
3. The threshold must be enforced with very few (if any) exceptions. Many schools we have worked with have communicated a threshold and have a clear decision maker, but ultimately do not enforce the cutoff with fidelity.

Combine sections across schools

An increasingly common strategy—and a good way to apply some of the remote instruction capacity developed during the pandemic—is for a teacher to teach a hybrid class that is received in person by students at one school and virtually by students in other schools. This approach can be especially effective for electives or AP courses with limited enrollment within a given school. A variation on this theme is to go all virtual, with the teacher on the computer in their classroom without any students physically present.

Ways to Make a Smoother Start

If you want to staff more precisely at your school or in your district, consider this final set of a few practical recommendations to move in this direction without too much pushback.

- **Move toward precise staffing over time.** As your school or district collects and examines more precise data about staffing and class-size inconsistencies, it can incrementally bring classes closer to enrollment targets. Making rapid and radical changes to course offerings and staffing, especially in schools or districts that traditionally have not tightly staffed to enrollment, can lead to significant pushback from teachers and parents alike.

- **Embrace attrition, not reduction in force (RIF) or involuntary transfers.** Sometimes the data reveals that a department is overstaffed by a full FTE. A budget hawk might be tempted to cut a teacher or transfer them to another school that needs a teacher. This can create a lot of blowback and sour folks on precision staffing. Taking a long view can build support for precision staffing. When a teacher in an overstaffed department leaves your school, do not fill the vacancy.

- **Use part-time or shared staff.** Often precise staffing calculations leads to the fact that a department needs, say, 8.4 teachers. Precision means that what is to the right of the decimal matters. Rounding up to full-time positions, in this case to 9.0, is a major reason for sections smaller than target class-size guidelines. If 8.4 FTE are needed, why not have 8 full-time folks and one 0.4 staff member in the building? Part-time positions and sharing staff are not common practices in many districts, but more and more districts are trying it and finding ways to make it work. See the next chapter about effective strategies for deploying part-time or shared staff.

◆ ◆ ◆

The school leaders, district leaders, and schedulers we have partnered with invariably work hard to staff thoughtfully and balance the needs of students, teachers, and the budget. Scheduling is not an easy task, especially at the high school level, but staffing to enrollment more precisely—down to the decimal place—can free up funds and provide additional, cost-free sections of intervention, electives, and other learning opportunities to students. It is worth the effort and will take the good work you are already doing another step forward.

In the next chapter, we will discuss additional ways that strategic scheduling can help you meet student needs and adhere to your budget.

All Levels, K–12

10

Strategic Scheduling and the Budget

*Learn how better schedules are also better
for the budget*

A few years ago, a district in New York reached out to us with an urgent request for support. The situation was grim: following a series of enrollment and funding changes, the district was facing a nearly $2 million budget gap—a substantial amount given the district's size. They were exploring ways to close the gap, including making across-the-board cuts, reducing transportation services, and cutting after-school programming. One thing the district was *not* closely looking at was school schedules.

A schedule represents the coordination of a school's single largest resource: its staff. Indeed, 90 percent of instructional expenditures in most districts can be attributed to staff salaries and benefits (Ellerson, 2011). How the schedule organizes staff time is one of the paramount decisions that schools and districts face and one that significantly affects the budget.

In the case of the New York district, we partnered with them and began to take a close look at their secondary schedules, conducting a detailed review of their course and staffing practices. Through more precise staffing and a careful review of secondary course offerings, the district was ultimately able to identify $1.7 million in potential savings without reducing learning opportunities for students or firing staff. The district went on to reduce staffing at most middle and high schools through natural attrition and by having shared and part-time staff fill what were previously full-time positions. On top of this, the process also helped the district realign some existing staffing and resources to expand academic intervention opportunities for students and incorporate more student voice and choice into the schedule process, both of which were strategic priorities of the district. This is a path more districts should explore, even those not in a budget crisis, and it is the focus of this chapter.

Three Ways to Save, Three Ways to Benefit

When we talk with educators about their schedules, we often ask, "If you could change just one thing about your school schedule, what would it be?" The two most common responses are "We need more time" and "We need more staff." The challenge to meeting both requests, of course, is that extending the school day and adding staff are cost-prohibitive for the majority of schools and districts. The politics and financial cost of extending the school day (or school year) make it a very difficult sell for most district leaders. Additional days or hours of learning are expensive, and changing the school schedule affects not only students and teachers but also parents, employers, and a wide range of businesses and industries that are dependent on the traditional school day and year.

Scheduling strategically, by comparison, does not require more money. Nor does it require a longer school day or more staff. What it does require is committing to using existing time in the day and current resources differently. This chapter looks at three powerful ways to schedule strategically that not only are good for the budget but can also benefit both teacher and student opportunities and outcomes:

1. Precisely match staffing to student enrollment by embracing part-time and shared staff.
2. Increase class size strategically (while maintaining support from stakeholders).
3. Reduce low-enrollment courses without reducing student choice.

Before we dive into these strategies and their benefits, here is another interesting way to think about the connection between the schedule and the budget. Let's say the imaginary Kennedy Middle School has 700 students and 48 teachers. The average combined salary and benefits for each teacher is $80,000, for total annual staffing costs of $3,840,000. The school year runs for 180 days, so the daily staffing cost of running the school is $21,333 per day. The school day runs for seven hours, so the hourly staffing cost is about $3,050 per hour, and the minute-by-minute staffing cost is therefore approximately $50 per minute. If we multiply the $50-per-minute staffing cost by 180 (the number of days in a typical school year), we learn that *every one minute* in the bell schedule equates to a $9,100 investment over the course of a year.

Is this how most educators think about schedules and budgets? Clearly not, and reasonably so. But the next time you are debating devoting a few thousand dollars for software licensing fees, remember that changing how teachers are scheduled by just one minute can be an equivalent investment!

Achieving More Precise Staffing with Part-Time and Shared Staff

In Chapter 9, we introduced a process that high schools (and middle schools too) can follow to calculate staffing needs based on student enrollment "to the decimal point." When the math works out to show a need for "fractional employees" (e.g., 6.3 FTE or 8.4 FTE), many schools will simply round up to the next FTE number and call it a day. Rounding up is common, but it is costly. Here are a few examples:

- A district of 5,000 students calculated precisely how many specialists they needed at each of its seven elementary schools. Most schools had either full-time or half-time PE, art, music, and library staff, and this level of staffing included a lot of rounding up. For example, while the district had a total of 6.5 FTE art teachers (five full-time and three part-time), it actually only needed 5.7 FTE, based on student enrollment. Precision staffing (that is, staffing down to the decimal place) saved $320,000 without reducing a single minute of the specials provided or increasing class size by a single student. The district reinvested these funds by hiring additional reading teachers, a service improvement.

- An 800-student middle school that staffed all noncore positions with full-time staff discovered that noncore classes were 20 percent smaller than core classes. By shifting to a precision-staffing approach with part-time staff, the school "got back" $375,000, which was repurposed to fund 4.0 FTE of mental health services.

- The principal of a large high school who scheduled 15 sections of Algebra 1 and 15 sections of Algebra 2 to "fill" the schedules of his six math teachers when only 24 sections total were actually needed had in fact "invested" about $100,000 in slightly smaller classes. Upon realizing this, the school added six sections of math intervention instead.

Exploring a precise staffing approach has an arguably undesirable side effect: school leaders learn that most departments do not need all 1.0 FTE staff. Many departments need one fractional position in order to staff precisely. We say *undesirable* because, historically, K–12 education has not easily or readily embraced part-time or shared staff. Traditionally, the teaching profession has required practitioners to be in-person, in front of students in the classroom, on a daily basis, all day long. Most educators in the past also wanted and expected full-time employment, and those who pursued part-time teaching or were shared between schools often did not have great experiences. They felt disconnected from their school. One teacher who worked in two buildings described herself as "a woman without a country." Another commented that splitting time between schools meant twice the meetings and half the friendships.

Fast forward to today. Many of the structural and historical reasons behind the preference for only full-time staff at schools still exist, but the willingness and interest of many to teach part-time is greater than ever. Other knowledge industries and professions, such as engineering, law, and consulting, have already picked up on this trend. It's true that shared and part-time staffing is not without some drawbacks, but a strategic scheduler recognizes that embracing and normalizing these practices is an effective way to add new courses, expand mental health services, and fund intervention. Given the growing teacher shortages, it is also a great way to tap into previously unexplored talent pools.

Use part-time staff or partial FTE

The shortage of teachers over the past decade has been acute in some subjects and accelerating in many districts on account of the pandemic. The shortage of teachers is one more reason to stop rounding up when it comes to staffing. A growing number of schools have found new teachers and staffed precisely by recruiting part-time staff.

One of these was a high school in Minnesota that had a tricky scheduling situation for 9th grade Algebra. The school projected it would have 200 students enrolled in Algebra and a target class size of 25 students. One full-time teacher could handle five sections, or 125 students total. That left three sections and 75 students—not enough to support hiring a second full-time math teacher. To address the situation, the school hired a recently retired business executive (who had taught high school math for 10 years earlier in her career) to teach the three remaining sections and work between 8:00 a.m. and 12:00 p.m. every day.

As schools search for teachers, they have found that many folks who do not apply to job postings for full-time roles are, in fact, interested in part-time positions. This includes retired teachers or former teachers with school-age children who cannot (or would prefer not to) commit to a full teaching load. Many of the same individuals, however, would gladly teach one section of AP Calculus, for example, or two sections of English 9. Additional folks who may find the option of part-time positions appealing include teachers who are returning from parental leave, pursuing a master's degree or doctorate, recovering from illness, nearing retirement, caring for elderly or disabled family members, or running a side business. It is important to note that teachers sourced from these pools need to be just that—trained, effective *teachers*. "Part-time" does not mean finding individuals with no teaching experience and allowing them to teach two sections of 6th grade math because they have the time. This only sets them and their students up for failure.

Trained and experienced part-time staff can be a great way to fill nonteaching roles as well, such as instructional coaches, counselors, social workers, and related services. Not only can this be great for the teacher, but many principals prefer "owning" a part-time teacher as opposed to sharing part of a full-time teacher split across schools. It is much easier to schedule a 0.6 FTE Spanish teacher that teaches only at your school, for example, than a 0.6 FTE Spanish teacher at your school that is also 0.4 FTE at another school.

Though many teachers are ready to jump at part-time positions, schools were designed with full-time staff in mind. But there are a number of best practices that can help your school become "part-time friendly." For example:

- Avoid rotational schedules (otherwise known as *waterfall schedules*), which vary the time of day when a course will be taught on a day-to-day basis.
- Include part-time staff in all communications, whole-day staff events, and whole-day school events. No one likes to be the person left out!
- Ensure participation in the coaching and evaluation cycle.
- Avoid assigning noninstructional responsibilities or duties (e.g., bus duty, lunch duty, study hall) that divert the teacher from maximizing their relatively limited time with students.
- Schedule faculty meetings and IEP meetings during the hours that part-time staff are in the building.

Retain teachers with young children

Imagine you are a 3rd grade teacher at an elementary school that starts its day at 7:30 a.m. You and your spouse recently welcomed a new child and are looking for childcare options. But none of the local childcare centers are open before 8:00 a.m. Worse yet, to get a spot in one of these centers, you must make a full 52-week commitment, even though you only need childcare for 36 weeks of the year. What do you do? Many teachers in this situation rely on a family member, spouse, or significant other to drop off their child(ren) in the morning. Others choose to stay home and drop out of the workforce.

Addressing the misalignments between childcare drop-off hours and school hours and between the school year and the 12-month work year is a potential opportunity for schools (especially at the elementary level, where the school day tends to start earlier) to recruit and retain teachers who are the parents of young children. Cost-free strategies that can help attract teachers caught in this conundrum and provide more flexible work options include the following:

- Restructuring morning duties to facilitate a later arrival for some staff two to three times a week, potentially on a rotational basis. This may include "trading time," such that if a teacher arrives later in the morning, they stay later in the afternoon.
- Exploring opportunities for compressed hours, late starts, early finishes, or virtual planning time from home.
- Partnering with a childcare provider to open a childcare site at the school campus. Doing so allows teachers to bring young children with them to school.

Minimize hassle for shared staff

Even if all teachers want full-time positions, you can still staff more precisely by sharing staff with another school. If you are thinking, *We already share staff and hate it*, please don't bail on us yet. Most principals we know wish and hope for fewer shared staff, and many shared staff long for a single school, but shared staffing does not have to be a negative experience for anyone. Just as schools need to be part-time friendly, they also need to be hassle-free for teachers who work at more than one school.

If there is just one thing to know about sharing staff, it is this: align bell schedules between schools that share staff. Failing to do so makes a shared staffing approach either very inefficient (due to missed instructional time) or helpful for one school but less helpful for the other school.

At the elementary level, unifying schedules across schools is the best way to increase the amount of time specials teachers have with students. As an all-too-common example, a district we partnered with had five elementary schools that shared music, art, and PE teachers. Each principal created their own schedule (the norm in most districts), which resulted in specials teachers traveling between schools mid-day, often arriving five minutes after a period started, thus waiting 40 minutes for the next block to start. The district needed to hire an additional specials teacher in each subject to cover gaps in the schedule.

Over the course of six months, the district worked with principals to agree on a common bell schedule, which allowed the schools to continue to share specials teacher but on a schedule that assigned each specials teacher to a school for a full day. The principals agreed to set a similar period length for specials (45 minutes) as well as a common specials rotation, which involved the two schools that previously ran specials on a four-day cycle agreeing to run specials on a five-day cycle to align to the other three schools. Doing so allowed specials teachers to avoid mid-day travel and provide more equitable specials courses and experiences for students at different campuses.

At the secondary level, it is fairly common for a middle and high school that are in close proximity (if not in the same facility) to share staff. Some specific examples would be

- A music teacher teaching Band at the high school and providing music lessons at the middle school.
- A French teacher providing instruction in two schools.
- A physics teacher at the high school also teaching a science elective for 8th graders.
- A 1.0 FTE math teacher teaching 0.4 hours at the high school and 0.4 hours at the middle school. Yes, 0.2 FTE is lost to travel, but this arrangement is more cost-effective than both schools rounding up.

Additionally, schools' pandemic-related experience with remote instruction has helped many educators be more open to sharing staff. One high school we partnered with, for example, allowed an ELA teacher at one high school to teach four sections of English 11 in person and one section of a creative writing elective remotely at a second, short-staffed district high school. The students enrolled in the creative writing class sat together in the same room, were supervised by a paraprofessional, and joined the teacher via Zoom. Each student had their own laptop and headphones so that they could fully participate in the lesson.

Regardless of the grade level, there are a few best practices for sharing staff that can help to minimize hassles for both the teachers and principals:

1. **Make sure every teacher or staff member who is shared has a "home" school, even if they are split evenly between two schools.** They should default to joining faculty meetings, participating in schoolwide events, and even attend the staff holiday party, all at their home school. Doing so helps ensure the shared staff member feels closely attached to at least one school instead of frustratingly afloat between two.

2. **Assign shared staff at the elementary level to just one school per day.** Eliminating mid-day travel saves significant time over the course of the school year and ensures shared staff maximize their time with students.

3. **Help shared staff avoid "double-meeting syndrome."** This is when staff members end up attending the same mandatory meeting at two different schools.

4. **Team up with partnering schools to build shared staff's schedules.** Schools that share staff need to build their schedules together, as a team. If each individual school schedules alone, hassles will abound.

Sharing staff can be a double-edged sword—very helpful but also restricting. If you find that scheduling shared staff limits your ability to achieve other scheduling priorities, then you may consider scaling back on shared staff to reduce schedule constraints and instead invest in part-time staff specific to your school. This happens most often when the fourth guideline above, scheduling in partnership, is skipped.

Find partial FTE who are hiding in plain sight

Another way to staff precisely is to consider providing full-time teachers a stipend to teach an additional section during what would normally be their planning period. This can be a quadruple win. The first win is "no rounding up"—you're not paying for an additional FTE. The second win is avoiding the hassle (and recruitment cost) of finding a part-time or shared teacher. The third win is more money in the existing teacher's pocket. Provided you offer the extra section to a highly effective teacher, the fourth win is more students learning from a great teacher.

One district was hesitant go this route, fearing it would overburden already-busy staff and increase burnout. They were surprised to learn that a third of the teachers on staff already had second jobs, and many jumped at the chance to teach an extra section and quit their after-school, summer, or weekend gig.

Making Strategic Class-Size Increases

We know from experience that class size is sometimes (well, usually) a hot topic among educators and parents. Perspectives vary regarding what the "right" class size is or should be. In Vermont, for example, 18 students in 1st grade seems huge, but in Minnesota, 24 1st graders in a class is on the small side. Many California high schools feel any class under 30 kids a is breeze, while in Massachusetts, 30 kids per class feels unmanageable. Despite this range, one thing that almost everyone can agree on is that smaller classes are preferred—or rather, it's preferred by everyone *except* for education researchers and the district business office.

There is a large body of research on the relationship between class size and student learning. As pointed out in Chingos and Whitehurst (2011), these studies have shown that class size has either only a small effect or no effect at all on student achievement. In other words: smaller class sizes do not typically lead to meaningful improvements in academic outcomes even though many educators, parents, and stakeholders think they do. To be fair, a small subset of studies found that dramatic class-size reductions, on the order of 7–10 fewer students per class, can have a meaningful long-term effect on student achievement, especially when introduced in elementary grades and for students from lower socioeconomic family backgrounds. Other studies found that an increase in the numbers of new and/or uncertified teachers hired to teach the larger number of classes offset much of these academic gains. Put another way, students who ended up in the classrooms of inexperienced teachers suffered academically from the teacher's inexperience by almost the same amount as they benefited from being in a smaller class.

With all that said, both of us are pragmatic people and recognize class size can be the third rail in many districts, despite the lack of consistent or compelling research about class-size reduction driving student achievement. That does not mean districts should not consider larger classes, just that they should do it in nuanced and politically aware ways. Use a fine-tip brush instead of a paint roller.

Fortunately, there are a number of strategies that savvy school and district leaders can apply to selectively increase class size, dramatically reduce pushback, and still make an meaningful difference on the budget and the schedule. We'll look at a few now.

Set nuanced class-size targets at the secondary level

A superintendent in Missouri once came to us with the following question: "How do I know if I have the 'right' number of staff at my high schools?" To help him answer this question, we conducted what we call a *course and staffing analysis,* examining in hyper-detail the different courses offered at schools, the enrollment of those courses, and who taught each course. Part of this analysis included comparing existing class-size figures to district class-size targets and determining whether the average class size across courses was above, below, or at district targets.

When we ran the numbers for this superintendent, we discovered that the existing class sizes at his high schools were in line with the district's class-size target of 25 students. The trouble was that the district only had one universal class-size target for all subjects and types of courses. So, for example, sections of Algebra 1 in 9th grade were supposed to be the same size as sections of AP Spanish in 12th grade, which were supposed to be the same size as sections of PE in 10th grade. While the district's high schools had the "right" number of staff according to the district class-size target, this one-size-fits-all target resulted in some classes (like PE) being smaller than the targets set in peer districts, and other classes (like Algebra 1) being larger than what some other thoughtful districts had—all of which resulted in a more expensive set of school schedules. A far better approach, we advised the district, would be to set more nuanced class-size targets.

Ultimately, the district kept the target class size of general-level core classes at the district-recommended 25 students but extended it to 28 students for honors and AP classes and most noncore elective classes. The class size for PE was set higher—at 40 students. Over the next several years, the average class size of noncore electives became larger than average core classes, and the district was able to save over $400,000 (through attrition), all without reducing the variety of courses available to students.

A similar strategy can work at middle schools, and even some elementary schools have found it easier to increase 4th and 5th grade classes so long as K–3 classrooms stay small.

Regroup and combine specials classes at the elementary level

Most elementary schools follow what we call the "1:1 specials rule"—each classroom is assigned to their own specials period. For example, if there are five classrooms of 22 students each in 3rd grade, each 3rd grade classroom typically has its own art period, music period, and so on. Instead of running five sections of specials for 3rd graders, one for each classroom, you could run just four sections and redistribute the students from the fifth classroom as evenly as possible. The various specials teachers would have a handful of additional students to teach, but you would need only four sections of 3rd grade art, music, PE, and so on. See Figure 10.1 for an illustration of how this can work. Alternatively, you can mix

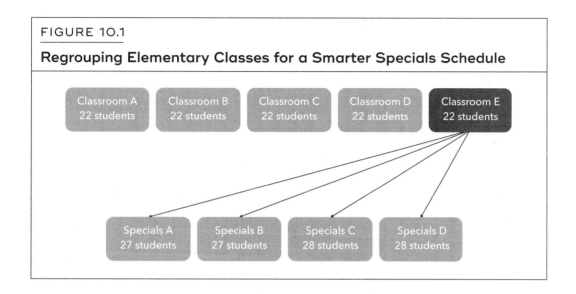

FIGURE 10.1

Regrouping Elementary Classes for a Smarter Specials Schedule

up all students in the grade and divide them into four specials classes instead of moving students from just one classroom into the other classrooms. Either option saves you 20 percent of the specials teachers needed in a school and increases students' range of socialization.

Incentivize top teachers to want larger classes

Imagine a rock star 1st grade teacher with impressive reading growth scores or a high school math teacher who makes the subject come alive for even the most math-challenged students. Wouldn't it be great if every student, or at least more students, had these teachers?

A growing number of schools are offering these highly effective teachers a sizable stipend to increase their class size by five to eight students. This can be a push-back-free way to increase class size. Parents like it because their child has a great teacher, and teachers like it because it is both optional and rewarded. A district in Louisiana that had difficulty finding content-strong teachers took this approach and was able to find the equivalent of 3.8 FTE across their schools by incentivizing existing effective teachers to teach an additional section.

"Oversize" select courses

Some classes really can be much, much bigger than the norm. At the high school level, consider oversizing select (though certainly not all) honors or AP/IB courses. The move toward early college and dual enrollment prompts us to note that high school Calculus typically has about 22 students, but the exact same class taught at college (mere months later) often has more than 100 students in a lecture hall.

At all grade levels, consider creating a few very large sections of PE. Many after-school sports, like cross country, have 60-plus athletes taught by a single coach, and it is a reasonable leap for many to see this ratio work in PE classes.

Reducing Low-Enrollment Courses but Preserving Student Choice

Even after creatively and precisely matching staffing to enrollment (as discussed in Chapter 9), many schools can (or need to) find other ways to maintain a variety of course offerings in a schedule.

One immutable budget fact is that it costs the same to teach a class of five students as it does a class of 25 students. About 20 percent of a teacher's salary goes to each course they teach. It is sad to see many school leaders wrestle with the Hobson's choice of "Do we keep a low-enrollment class because some students really want it, or do we cut that course to help balance the budget?" The good news is that there is a plethora of options for schedulers to consider that will help schools effectively manage low-enrollment courses without reducing student choice. Expert schedulers recognize that course management is much more than just saying "yes" or "no" to a course; it includes creatively adjusting the course's frequency, duration, and content in ways that preserve the course while increasing its enrollment.

Take a high school in Virginia we helped. Every term, the high school ran 154 low-enrollment courses, which represented approximately a third of all class offerings. Many of these low-enrollment courses were offered as a single section. District leadership, school leadership, and the community were all very proud of the variety of courses and choices available to their students. "Our students deserve to have these options!" was a common refrain. What was less commonly discussed, however, was the cost and opportunity cost to the high school of regularly running so many low-enrollment courses, some of which had only eight or nine students. The de facto investment on the part of the school to run so many low-enrollment courses was $2.5 million, or the equivalent of the 31.0 FTE. Worse than the extra dollars spent was that the school could not afford much intervention staff, behavior supports, or mental health counseling. Every dollar spent in one way means it cannot be spent elsewhere.

When confronted with these figures, school and district leaders thought they faced two options: either reduce the number of courses offered to students (not ideal from the community's perspective) or continue to invest significant amounts of money on low-enrollment offerings (not ideal from the budget's perspective). As we helped them discover, there was a third path forward: strategic course management.

There are seven practical and cost-free ways to manage low-enrollment courses without reducing options for students. Some of these are briefly noted in Chapter 9, but we will provide an expanded discussion here.

Alternate course offerings by quarter, semester, or year

Not all courses need to run every term or year. Many elementary and middle schools, for example, rotate what specials or unified art classes students take on a quarterly basis. High schools can run low-enrollment electives every other semester or year. For example, creative writing may run during the fall term, but not the spring, increasing enrollment to a more typical class size and "saving" a section. Some schools offer elective courses (e.g., Forensic Science, Math in Media, Computer Science Principles, Music Appreciation) on a two-year rotation. There are also high schools that have chosen to offer certain advanced placement courses every-other-year. Doing so boosts enrollment for courses that may otherwise only have 10 or 11 students but still allows students to take these AP courses during their high school career.

Combine similar courses

Consider combing related low-enrollment courses. For example, if one teacher normally teaches Journalism and Introduction to Podcasting, these courses can be combined to create Media Studies. While some kids are recording or editing a podcast, others might be learning about writing for the news media. A few more combinations we have seen at the high school level include Creative Writing and Advanced Creative Writing, Yoga and Wellness, and Water Colors and Oil Painting.

Combine levels of the same subject

Explore mixing the enrollment of two different levels of a course if they each have low enrollment. This strategy can work for electives, like Accounting 1 and 2, as well as for sequential courses, such as French 3 and 4. Be sure to consult with the teachers potentially affected, however, and ask for volunteers first.

Combining or mixing courses by level can be heretical for teachers unaccustomed to the practice, but it represents an exciting opportunity for others. One very small high school in Massachusetts offered five different foreign languages, all through the AP level—an impressive set of offerings indeed. Participation in foreign language was very strong, and student outcomes were equally impressive; as a result, the school was able to attract experienced foreign language teachers who were up for the challenge and thrived on the opportunity.

Evaluate the need for multi-section courses

Often, offering multiple sections of extra-small courses is the result of trying to meet student preferences elsewhere in their schedule. While the intent is admirable, the practice is expensive and may result in other students being denied extra support because teachers that otherwise could provide intervention are tied up teaching multiple sections of the same course.

Carefully evaluate whether Spanish 1, for example, really needs five sections averaging 19 students per class. Could 19 of these students be redistributed to give you four sections of 23 or 24 students? See Chapter 9 for guidance on how to determine which courses may need fewer sections.

Offer independent studies

Consider providing students with unique or very specific interests the opportunity to engage in formal independent study. The student uses one period each day for the independent study and meets with a teacher once a week during a teacher planning period. As an example, a 12th grade student at a high school we worked signed up for an independent study with the teacher who taught him Physics in 11th grade rather than enroll in AP Chemistry. He studied the physics of golf throughout his senior year and ended up pursuing mechanical engineering in college.

Switch some elective courses to extracurricular clubs

Evaluate whether it makes sense to switch an elective course like Photography 1 to a before-school or after-school club. This option may be beneficial for unique courses with relatively low enrollment but a passionate set of students interested in the topic.

Shift some courses to remote instruction

Both advances in technology and teachers' and students' increased experience and comfort with virtual instruction means it's more feasible than ever to offer select courses online. Courses with very low enrollment can be combined across campuses and taught by a teacher at a single school. One district that took this approach was able to save the cost of bussing all middle school students taking an advanced math course across town to a common location. Now, students simply log on and join the class from their home school.

◆ ◆ ◆

It might be easy to walk away from this chapter with the impression that strategic scheduling is only about finding efficiencies and saving money. Let us be clear: while important considerations for any scheduler, scheduling efficiently and in a budget-friendly way must be *in service of* students and staff, not ends in themselves.

In the next and final chapter, we discuss an often-overlooked aspect of strategic scheduling: ways you can improve the process of schedule construction. It's very hard to build an excellent schedule without an excellent process—one that considers timing, who is at the scheduling table, and the decision-making rules. Read on, and you won't be disappointed.

11

A Smarter Scheduling Process

A better process leads to better schedules

We shared at the beginning of the book that we rarely hear educators talking about how much they love their schedule. When talking with teachers, it is much more common for us to hear comments along the lines of "It is so frustrating that my schedule changes every year." And from principals, we hear "I just do not have enough staff to build the schedule my students need." Although many folks complain about their schedule, the real source of their dissatisfaction is often the problematic scheduling process that created it.

"The Scheduling Process"

What do we mean by *the scheduling process*? It is not a term or subject that gets discussed much, yet the only way to get a great schedule is by following a great scheduling process. At the heart of it are a few essential understandings and a lot of decisions, including

- Differentiating between who will decide what is in a schedule and who will actually build the schedule—activities that require different skillsets.
- Deciding which tools will be used to build the schedule (e.g., dedicated software, Microsoft Excel, Post-It notes).

- Deciding how staffing levels and the mix of staff will be determined.
- Establishing an order for how decisions will be made.
- Determining what freedoms and guardrails the scheduling team will have.
- Determining when and how scheduling decisions will be made.

In our experience, the scheduling process is the most overlooked opportunity to support the creation of strategic schedules. In fact, it is not uncommon for schools to come to us and say, "We need a new schedule!" when what they really need is an improved process to create their schedule. From our work with, and study of, schools and districts that manage their scheduling process especially well, there are steps that stand out. In this chapter, we will look more deeply at the elements of each step of the strategic scheduling process.

Step 1: Approach Scheduling as a Team Sport

Creating a great schedule is hard. No one person has all the wisdom, expertise, authority, and data necessary to build the best schedule by themselves. What's more, changing a schedule from something that is traditional, cumbersome, inefficient, and inequitable can be a political minefield. Excluding important stakeholders—especially teachers—from scheduling discussions can easily undermine support for a new and better schedule.

The tale of two hardworking principals exemplifies the value of approaching scheduling from this angle.

Principal A, who headed up a middle school in Texas, took a "go it alone" approach. He waited until the summer to think about the schedule so that he did not burden any of his staff. (Their time, he reasoned, was better spent preparing for the school year and enjoying summer vacation.) Principal A reviewed the district guidance about the schedule and, while he had a few questions and concerns—among them, class-size targets for electives and the fact that he had more world language teachers than he wanted and not enough intervention staff as he'd hoped for—he did the best he could with the hand he was dealt. Over the summer, he spent two full weeks building the schedule by himself. When he was finished, Principal A was proud that many kids got their first-choice electives, although he wondered why this number was lower than it had been in the past. He added an advisory block and was generally pleased with the schedule, all things considered.

Few shared his satisfaction. Teachers balked at the advisory period, uncertain how best to use the time, and all lamented the lack of intervention. Ultimately, the schedule had to be reworked by the school counselor a week prior to school opening, which was a significant stressor for staff (to put it mildly). The advisory program was halted mid-year due to low investment from both students and staff.

Principal B, a middle school principal in Missouri, took a team approach to building the schedule. The work began in January, when she recruited a mix of staff members for a scheduling design committee that reviewed the current schedule during the spring and identified improvements to make for the following school year. Principal B recognized the limit of her authority as a school leader and partnered with the district's chief of schools to discuss specific frustrations she had with some scheduling constraints, such as how shared staff were scheduled and the resulting effect on common planning time. Over the summer, she worked collaboratively with the chief of schools and other principals with whom she shared staff and created additional sections of intervention for students by getting permission to fill a vacancy with an interventionist rather than the role identified in the budget. Principal B knew her time was best spent setting a vision for the schedule, not building the schedule herself, so she asked a school counselor who had expertise in scheduling to take on this role—and provided a small stipend for compensation.

The resulting schedule was shared with students and staff two weeks prior to the start of the year, and Principal B was able to use part of the professional development days prior to the school's opening to share a clear vision for the year ahead.

Did both schools wind up with a schedule? Yes. But the superior schedule—the one that was better for students and teachers—emerged from the team effort. On paper, both schedules had effective elements, such as advisory and time for academic intervention, but only the schedule at Principal B's school aligned with her vision and was created in such a way that set students and teachers up for success.

Who should be on a scheduling team?

The most successful teams are composed of the following members performing the following roles:

- **The district's assistant superintendent of teaching and learning,** who sets the overall direction, goals, and priorities for schedules across schools in the district; provides scheduling guidelines and parameters; and can be called on to remove obstacles and clarify constraints.
- **The school principal,** who sets the school's scheduling direction, goals, and priorities and works closely with the district assistant superintendent of teaching and learning to align on a vision.
- **A guidance counselor/assistant principal,** who manages the logistics of the scheduling process and keeps things on track.
- **General education teachers,** preferably teaching core subject(s), who provide input on scheduling decisions and tradeoffs from the perspective of general education instruction.
- **A special education or English learner teacher,** who provide inputs on scheduling decisions and tradeoffs from the perspective of student supports.
- **An expert scheduler,** either school-based or district-based, who uses specialized scheduling software to build student and teacher schedules.

Thoughts on team composition

Some principals reading this might be surprised, disappointed even, that there is a prominent role for the central office on the scheduling team. We have seen many principals guard their schedule as a school-based responsibility; however, these are generally the same folks who do not love their schedule.

Very often, scheduling is driven by a lot of "myths" about what is and is not a priority and what is and is not possible. When we ask principals why their school's schedule is designed a certain way (typically a way that seems at odds with best practices), it is not uncommon to hear "That's what the district wants" or "We are required to do it that way." When we ask whether certain options to refine the schedule have been explored, common refrains include "The contract will not allow it" or "There is no way that is possible in this district."

In other words, principals often see a lot of obstacles to building strategic schedules—obstacles they feel are imposed from above. What is fascinating is that more often than not, the district would be fine with the changes these principals want to make, but no one asked. In some cases, the obstacles never existed to begin with; they were myths built on misunderstanding the preferences of long-retired former leaders. In other cases, the requirements were real but could have been altered for a good reason. Schools seldom build strategic schedules without central office support.

The other surprise on reading the scheduling team membership list is the limited role of specials or noncore teachers. To be sure, specials and noncore classes matter a lot, but do they matter *more* than core classes? Based on what we have seen, it is typical for scheduling teams to give much *less* voice to core teachers compared to noncore ones. Here is how it happens.

Hoping to ensure fairness in the scheduling process, each department gets one representative. This often means staff from art, music, PE, guidance, family and consumer science, special education services, and English language learning all have a seat at the scheduling table. They have the numbers to "outvote" representatives from the four core subjects. Some smaller scheduling teams have just two core teachers and a few noncore representatives, but if there is no math teacher at the table, math intervention typically gets much less support. Just as a schedule should reflect school priorities, so should the relative mix of members on the scheduling team.

Step 2: Set Clear Priorities and Identify the Non-Negotiables

"If you don't know where you are going, any path will take you there." This paraphrase of a conversation in Lewis Carroll's *Alice in Wonderland* is a great summary of how scheduling is too often conducted. Scheduling teams start to build a schedule and then squabble over each decision, because they skipped the key step of first agreeing on what is most important.

When trying to surface the true priorities, it can help to survey students and staff. **Appendix D (see p. 205) provides a survey template that invites teachers to comment on how well the current schedule is working for them and their students.** Based on input like this, many scheduling teams create long lists of what they would like to see in their schedule, and each item is a worthy goal. The problem, of course, is that you cannot have 10 "first priorities." Strategic schedules require a *prioritized* list of priorities.

A recommended prioritization process

Here is how we encourage scheduling teams to go about this work.

First, based on feedback on the current schedule and an assessment of student needs, brainstorm a preliminary, unnumbered list of priorities. For a middle school, the first list might look something like this:

Preliminary Scheduling Priorities

- A double block of ELA is offered for 6th grade students.
- Staff receive common grade-level content planning time every day.
- Students who struggle with reading are enrolled in a reading intervention course.
- Science teachers have common planning time 4th period.
- All students take a world language every day.
- Intervention courses are taught by content-strong teachers.

Now comes the hard part: splitting the preliminary list into a list of must-haves (up to four items) and a list of nice-to-haves (the rest). Once that's done, rank-order both lists from most valued to least critical. For example:

"Must Have" Priorities

1. All students who struggle with reading are enrolled in a reading intervention course.
2. Intervention courses are taught by content-strong teachers.
3. Staff get common planning time with their department.

"Nice to Have" Priorities

4. A double block of ELA is offered for 6th graders.
5. All students take a world language class every day.
6. Science teachers have common planning time 4th period.

Having a clear set of "must have" priorities helps the school scheduler navigate potentially tricky tradeoffs. It also makes the decisions behind schedule building more transparent. For example, there will be no surprise and less pushback when the scheduler cannot give science teachers common planning time during 4th period (Priority 6) if doing so would conflict with ensuring common department planning time for all staff (Priority 3). Even a much-desired double block of ELA (Priority 4) might be omitted if English teachers are needed to ensure all intervention courses are taught by content-strong staff (Priority 2).

In parallel to determining priorities, the scheduling team should also identify non-negotiables and other schedule parameters. Sometimes non-negotiables are driven by teacher or staff contracts (e.g., teachers must have at least one prep period daily). Other times, non-negotiables are related to teaching and learning best practices that should be incorporated into the schedule for the benefit of students. Common categories of non-negotiables include the following:

- Teacher contract hours and workload
- Time committed to phonics instruction
- Annual hours devoted to core subjects
- Prohibitions on reading and math pullouts
- Intervention in one subject for all struggling students from content-strong staff.

A district's responsibility to define "loose" versus "tight" schedule parameters

A core responsibility of the district during the scheduling process is to set schedule parameters that define the boundaries within which schools must operate. "Tight" parameters are those that are the same (or very similar) across all schools and meant to ensure consistency and ease of coordination. Examples include the start and end times of the school day, the length of the reading block at the elementary level, and how many hours of math instruction a student receives each year. "Loose" parameters give individual campuses more leeway. Examples include the length of the lunch period, the length of between-class transitions, and the electives offered.

Certain loose parameters can—or should—still have guidelines. For example, a school may decide to run six or seven periods (but not eight) or run 50- or 60-minute periods (but not 70-minute ones). Keep in mind that the fewer tight parameters and more loose parameters individual schools have, the more difficult it will be to share staff and align services between schools.

Step 3: Align the Scheduling Process with Staffing and Budgeting Timelines

Schedules are not built in a vacuum. They are greatly influenced by staffing and budgeting decisions and can greatly affect staffing and budgeting decisions in return.

One Pennsylvania district we worked with had a typical order of operations. Preliminary budget and staffing information was shared with principals in early winter, *before* course offerings were finalized by the school and students selected their desired courses. This resulted in schools having too many teachers in some departments while not enough in other departments. Many schools did not have enough teachers for their most in-demand electives or enough interventionists.

To prevent these challenges, the district convened a cross-department team to document key activities across the scheduling, budgeting, and staffing processes and map them in one chart (see Figure 11.1 for an example). They then rearranged the order in which things happened. Student course selections and estimates of the

FIGURE 11.1

A Timeline of the Scheduling Process

1	Establish scheduling teams, including member-specific roles and responsibilities.	October
2	Document and discuss successes and challenges of current schedule.	November
3	Establish scheduling priorities and non-negotiables.	December
4	Set scheduling process timeline and milestones.	December
5	Finalize course offerings/course catalog.	December
6	Draft a master bell schedule that blocks of time and collect feedback from staff.	January
7	Collect student course preferences (if applicable).	February–March
8	Project section and course loads to determine staffing needs.	March
9	Draft the master schedule in scheduling software.	April
10	Update the master schedule as staffing, budget, and student preference data is finalized, and share preliminary course assignments with staff.	April–July
11	Set regular meetings as the scheduling team to discuss/navigate tradeoffs as they arise.	April–July
12	Share schedules with students and staff.	August
13	Incorporate training on new components of the schedule into staff days prior to the start of the school year.	August

number of students needing intervention came first. Draft schedules were next, and budgeting and staffing decisions followed after that. Schedules were finalized based on the budget decisions, but the final schedules closely resembled the desired ones.

Step 4: Use Expert Schedulers

Building great schedules requires both a great plan as well as an expert scheduler to bring the plan to life. One without the other leads to frustration and missed opportunities.

David's first experience building a school schedule was not that different from the experience of many school administrators new to the role. He received a large Microsoft Excel file (the previous year's master schedule document) and did his best to update it so it reflected the names of current staff members. Although he successfully maintained the status quo, he did not exactly create a master schedule that was aligned to any set of priorities, let alone to student needs. The following year, with a bit more experience under his belt and the help of another administrator in the district who had significant scheduling expertise, David was able to update his school's schedule and incorporate significantly more enrichment time for students (a goal of the school's that year).

What David learned from his experience as the owner of a middle school schedule is that *designing* a schedule (i.e., determining what to schedule) takes a different set of skills than *building* a schedule (i.e., creating the actual schedules of staff and students on paper or in a software program). Designing a schedule requires teamwork, as we have noted; building a schedule that maximizes student choice and staff reach requires a certain degree of technical expertise. When schools or districts rely on inexperienced or untrained school leaders to build schedules, they do so at their own peril.

The toll they pay is often in time (not to mention a less-then-ideal schedule for students). In our work with schools, school leaders share comments like "Our process is still very manual and takes a *long* time. We always seem to be re-doing the schedule" and "We are able to create schedules that meet the needs of our students, but it is very, very cumbersome and time-consuming." Luckily, there is a better way to approach building schedules, and it's to use an expert.

The skills you're looking for

Expert schedulers can ensure student needs and requests are met, that staff are used efficiently, and that the schedule aligns with the leaders' vision and priorities. There are a few skills any expert scheduler should bring to the table. For a sample job description of a district-level expert scheduler, see Figure 11.2.

FIGURE 11.2

A Job Description for a District-Level Expert Scheduler

_____ Public Schools seeks a Master Scheduler to join its team. The Master Scheduler is the district's point person for coordinating, improving, and supporting scheduling at each school at the elementary, middle, and high school levels. This person in this position will be responsible for assisting school-based staff and leaders in building master schedules that support teaching and learning best practices, school and district goals, and financial efficiency. Responsibilities also include developing and refining standardized protocols and templates for future scheduling. The Master Scheduler must be able to take ownership of challenges, work collaboratively with others, and develop school-based capacity with a minimal supervision.

Position: Master Scheduler

Reports to: Chief Academic Officer, Assistant Superintendent for teaching and Learning or Chief Schools Officer (or equivalent)

Responsibilities and Duties

1. **Schedule Design and Construction**
   - Managing, coordinating, and supporting the creation of the master schedule and related student course requests and necessary staffing plans in close collaboration with school-based staff and leaders.
   - Identifying common challenges to building student-centered, financially efficient schedules and proposing feasible solutions.
   - Ensuring equitable access to courses and learning opportunities to students at all levels of need.
   - Working independently while appropriately escalating issues to school and district leaders based on identified priorities and non-negotiables.

2. **Training, Support, and Resources**
   - Leading or supporting schedule visioning and priority-setting discussions with school and district leaders.
   - Creating training resources and running reports that help school-based staff and leaders make informed and strategic decisions about school schedules and staffing.
   - Creating standard templates, processes, and timelines for schedule design.

3. **Continuous Improvement**
   - Identifying and prioritizing areas of improvement within current scheduling process.
   - Working with school leaders and district staff to adjust school schedules mid-year, as needed.
   - Producing annual reports (e.g., class-size averages, enrollment averages) for school and district leaders to reference.

(continued on next page)

FIGURE 11.2

A Job Description for a District-Level Expert Scheduler (*continued*)

Required Skill Set

The Master Scheduler will possess many of the following characteristics and qualifications:

- Strong technical skills. Competent with MS Excel and experience with _____ scheduling software.
- Strong interpersonal skills.
- Ability to work independently and analyze situations accurately to adopt an effective course of action.
- Ability to prioritize many important demands and rationalize the tradeoffs that come with different decisions.
- Ability to communicate effectively both orally and in writing.

Terms of Employment: This is a part-time position. Some weeks will require many more hours than others. Some weeks will require no hours at all.

First, the expert scheduler should be intimately familiar with any scheduling software, tools, or process the school uses to build its schedule. Similar to how providing a novice carpenter with a high-end set of tools will not lead to a masterfully created cabinet, offering an inexperienced scheduler access to top-of-the-line scheduling software will not guarantee a strategically designed schedule. Skill with the scheduling tools is a must.

Second, the expert scheduler should be very familiar with goals and priorities established by the scheduling team. Without this understanding, the expert scheduler will have little guidance for how to navigate the inevitable tradeoffs associated with building schedules.

Third, the expert scheduler should be able to work with the scheduling team to establish a clear escalation protocol to resolve the issues or tradeoffs that arise during the scheduling process. An escalation protocol is a plan for bringing sticking points or particular challenges about the schedule to a higher authority. Sometimes, an expert scheduler may not be able to meet an identified non-negotiable because of a limitation or constraint that is beyond their authority to resolve.

And fourth, the expert scheduler should be able to partner with the scheduling team to establish and communicate a policy regarding teacher scheduling requests. Some schedulers we work with regularly share that it's not uncommon for them to receive unsolicited requests from teachers such as, "Can you make sure I have 5th period off?" or "Can you try to schedule my classes in the morning?" Because most teachers seldom see the bigger scheduling picture, however, they are not aware of the broader impact complying with requests like these can have. Ensuring planning time during 5th period, for example, may mean that science teachers will not have access to common planning time and that a previously planned reading intervention period will not be feasible.

Where to find an expert scheduler

The good news is that an expert scheduler can be found in many places. Here are our recommendations:

- **Look inside the school.** Sometimes an expert scheduler is hiding in plain sight. Rather than assume that the expertise aligns to title (principal, assistant principal, guidance counselor), ask your staff. At some schools, it is a math or science teacher who builds the schedule and receives a stipend of a few thousand dollars to do so.
- **Look to other principals in the district.** Not every principal is an expert scheduler, but some are. A growing number of districts are asking the principal of one school to take the lead in scheduling other schools.
- **Look to other district resources.** Some districts employ a full- or part-time scheduling expert to support schools or identify a particular district leader or particular school-based staff member with the necessary expertise.
- **Hire an expert.** There are a small number of individual consultants and scheduling "gurus" who help build schedules for a living. Talk with local or peer districts to see if they use an outside partner.

• **Get software and an expert as a package for secondary schools.** Many expert schedulers are linked to a particular software package. It is unfortunately common for the outside expert you have identified and want to work with not be familiar with the program your school uses. A few firms do package scheduling software with expert support and training. Just keep in mind that if someone is not an expert scheduler, new software will not make them one.

Step 5: Train Staff on New Schedule Components and Provide Ongoing Support

The final key step in the strategic scheduling process is to ensure teachers and staff having the training and support necessary to implement the schedule as intended. If you are making changes to your schedule—adding an advisory period or an intervention block, say—be sure to codify and share your vision for how any new period of time should be used, from both the student perspective as well as the teacher perspective. Adding an intervention block, for example, requires detailing exactly what intervention will look like (i.e., who is teaching it, who is planning it, which curriculum is being used, and how students are assigned to it) and what students who are *not* assigned to intervention will do during that period (e.g., enrichment).

If you are switching schedule models from, say, a seven-period traditional schedule to an A/B block schedule, it is important to provide training for the new schedule as a multi-year effort. This might include training teachers on how to effectively teach in a 90-minute block (instead of a 50-minute period) during the school year and summer *before* the switch, conducting ample training and coaching during the first year of implementation, and providing regular "how to teach in a block schedule" professional development sessions for teachers new to the school. Some schools also decide to pilot a new schedule for a week multiple months before the full rollout. It's a way to give teachers and students a chance to experience the new schedule, identify and address any pain points or flaws in it, and provide some assurance to those not yet on board that the new plan will work.

◆ ◆ ◆

Schools that build strategic schedules by using a strategic scheduling process really can build budget-friendly, sustainable schedules that serve both students and staff and that both students and staff will love.

As you set off on your own scheduling journey, remember that you can schedule anything, just not everything. A strategic schedule is one that is aligned to your students' needs, the talents of your staff, the priorities of your school, and the realities of your context. What is strategic for your school may be a poor fit for the school down the street. Invest the time with your team at the beginning of the schedule-design process to prioritize your priorities and establish the schedule as a powerful tool to transform educational outcomes for your students. Good luck!

Appendix A

Elementary School Strategic Schedule Self-Assessment

Best Practice	Does your schedule include these best practices?		
	Definitely Yes	**Sometimes**	**Not Really**
1. All the minutes of the recommended time blocks add up to equal the length of the school day.			
2. Reading and math time blocks align with the curriculum developer's recommendations.			
3. There are micro-schedules for reading blocks.			
4. Reading and math blocks are staggered throughout the day.			
5. There is a 30-minute block for daily intervention and enrichment.			
6. Intervention time is common across a grade level.			
7. Intervention is staggered across grade levels throughout the day.			
8. Before- or after-school intervention is avoided.			
9. There is dedicated time for SEL and relationship-building activities.			
10. Specials (art, music, PE, etc.) staffing allow for the first nine best practices.			

Appendix B

Middle School Strategic Schedule Self-Assessment

Best Practice	Does your schedule include these best practices?		
	Definitely Yes	Sometimes	Not Really
1. Core subjects meet for at least 250 minutes a week (5 periods × 50 minutes).			
2. All students who need extra help in reading, math, or ELA receive extra help in at least the area of need.			
3. Extra help is extra time, one period a day, and focuses on one subject.			
4. Extra help is provided by teachers with deep content expertise.			
5. All students with the requisite skills are provided accelerated math in 7th and 8th grade.			
6. No student currently lacking the requisite math skills has been placed in accelerated math (including Algebra 1) in 8th grade.			
7. Student voice (passions/interests) is reflected in the non-core offerings.			
8. Students have some choice over non-core courses.			

Best Practice	Does your schedule include these best practices?		
	Definitely Yes	Sometimes	Not Really
9. Advisory and other relationship-building efforts have a foundation of shared interests between student and teacher.			
10. Staff and leadership believe strategic middle school schedules and the middle school model can coexist.			

Appendix C

High School Strategic Schedule Self-Assessment

Best Practice	Does your schedule include these best practices?		
	Definitely Yes	Sometimes	Not Really
1. Core subjects meet for at least 250 minutes a week (5 × 50 min.).			
2. All students with designated need in reading, math, or writing are enrolled in at least one content-specific, credit-bearing intervention course.			
3. Content-specific intervention courses run daily (as a "skinny" period if a block schedule) and focus on one subject.			
4. Intervention courses are taught by teachers with deep content expertise.			
5. Departments offer a broad mix of course levels (general, honors, advanced) to meet the needs and challenge students of all skill levels.			
6. Prerequisites ensure all students equitable access to courses and do not disproportionately screen out certain student demographic groups.			

Best Practice	Does your schedule include these best practices?		
	Definitely Yes	Sometimes	Not Really
7. Student voice (passions/interests) is reflected in elective offerings.			
8. Robust career and technical courses, early college (dual credit) courses, and internships in the community are available to students.			
9. Advisory and other relationship-building efforts have a foundation of shared interests between student and teacher.			
10. Staff and leadership believe a strategic high school schedule is a tool for—not a barrier to—student learning.			

Appendix D

What Do Teachers Think About the Current Schedule?
A Survey

Name:

Role:

Grade level(s) served:

1. Please rate the current schedule's overall impact on your students in the following areas:

	Negative	Neutral	Positive
Academic achievement			
Overall workload			
Engagement in class			
Attendance			
Ability to build strong relationships with teachers			
Ability to build strong relationships with other students			

2. Please rate the overall effectiveness of how the current schedule uses time in the following areas:

Course Offerings	Strongly Disagree	Disagree	Agree	Strongly Agree
Provides ample opportunity for students to take a variety of courses (e.g., electives, non-credit courses, half-credit courses)				
Allows opportunity for student voice in determining potential course offerings				
Allows flexibility and student choice (i.e., students can take courses that interest them)				

206 IT'S TIME FOR STRATEGIC SCHEDULING

Learning Time	Strongly Disagree	Disagree	Agree	Strongly Agree
Provides sufficient instructional time during each period for quality learning activities				
Provides sufficient opportunities for academic intervention during the school day				
Provides sufficient opportunities for social-emotional support and relationship building during the school day				

Teacher Time	Strongly Disagree	Disagree	Agree	Strongly Agree
Provides adequate planning and collaboration time for teachers				
Creates reasonable course prep requirements workloads for teachers				
Provides reasonable student caseloads for teachers				

3. Please rate the overall level and effectiveness of support and access in the current schedule:

	Strongly Disagree	Disagree	Agree	Strongly Agree
Ensures all students equitable access to rigorous course work				
Provides all students with opportunities to seek challenge				
Ensures that students who are English learners receive sufficient support during the school day				
Ensures that students with disabilities receive sufficient support during the school day				

4. Please rate how well the current schedule supports students' path to graduation:

	Strongly Disagree	Disagree	Agree	Strongly Agree
Allows every student to graduate on time with the required number of credits or more				
Ensures flexibility and student choice in the exploration of their interests and career pathways				
Provides student access to opportunities outside school (e.g., job, internship, college course)				

5. What are the greatest benefits of the current schedule? Please explain.

6. What are the greatest challenges of the current schedule? Please explain.

7. If you could change only one thing about the current schedule, what would you change? Please explain.

8. Please provide any additional feedback on the current schedule that you think would be helpful.

References

Aronson, J., Zimmerman, J., & Carlos, L. (1998, April). *Improving student achievement by extending school: Is it just a matter of time?* WestEd. https://www2.wested.org/www-static/online_pubs/po-98-02.pdf

Barshay, J. (2021, April 26). Proof points: Later school start time gave small boost to grades but big boost to sleep, new study finds. *The Hechinger Report.* https://hechingerreport.org/proof-points-later-school-start-time-gave-small-boost-to-grades-but-big-boost-to-sleep-new-study-finds/

Benner, M., Brown, C., & Jeffrey, A. (2019, August 4). *Elevating student voice in education.* Center for American Progress. https://www.americanprogress.org/article/elevating-student-voice-education/

Blackburn, B. (2013). *The beginner's guide to understanding rigor.* https://www.barbarablackburnonline.com/rigor/

Brenneman, R. (2016, March 23). Gallup student poll finds engagement in school dropping by grade level. *Education Week.* https://www.edweek.org/leadership/gallup-student-poll-finds-engagement-in-school-dropping-by-grade-level/2016/03

Centers for Disease Control and Prevention. (2019). *School connectedness.* https://www.cdc.gov/healthyyouth/protective/school_connectedness.htm

Chingos, M. M., & Whitehurst, G. J. R. (2011, May 11). *Class size: What research says and what it means for state policy.* Brookings Institution. https://www.brookings.edu/research/class-size-what-research-says-and-what-it-means-for-state-policy/

Clay, A., Chu, E., Altieri, A., Deane, Y., Lis-Perlis, A., Lizarraga, A., Monz, L., Muhammad, J., Recinos, D., Tache, J. A., & Wolters, M. (2021, May 4). *About time: Master scheduling and equity.* Center for Public Research and Leadership (CPRL) at Columbia University. https://cprl.law.columbia.edu/content/about-time-master-scheduling-and-equity

Corley, L. (2022, June 14). Q&A with retiring Bibb Schools Superintendent Curtis Jones. *The Macon Newsroom.* https://macon-newsroom.com/13719/news/local/qa-with-retiring-bibb-schools-superintendent-curtis-jones/

Dunster, G. P., de la Iglesia, L., Ben-Hamo, M., Nave, C., Fleischer, J. G., Panda, S., & de la Iglesia, H. O. (2018, December 12). Sleepmore in Seattle: Later school start times are associated with more sleep and better performance in high school students. *Science Advances, 4*(12). https://www.science.org/doi/10.1126/sciadv.aau6200#:~:text=The%20Seattle%20(WA)%20School%20District,devices%20(Actiwatch%20Spectrum%20Plus%2C%20Philips

Ellerson, N. (2011). *School budgets 101.* American Association of School Administrators. https://www.aasa.org/uploadedfiles/policy_and_advocacy/files/schoolbudgetbrieffinal.pdf

Farbman, D., & Kaplan, C. (2005). *Time for a change: The promise of extended-time schools for promoting student achievement.* Massachusetts 2020. https://files.eric.ed.gov/fulltext/ED534912.pdf

Gersten, R., Compton, D., Connor, C. M., Dimino, J., Santoro, L., Linan-Thompson, S., & Tilly, W. D. (2008). *Assisting students struggling with reading: Response to Intervention and multi-tier intervention for reading in the primary grades. A practice guide* (NCEE 2009-4045). National Center for Education Evaluation and Regional Assistance, Institute of Education Sciences, U.S. Department of Education. http://ies.ed.gov/ncee/wwc/publications/practiceguides/

Grossman, P. (2021, March 11). Want to improve learning outcomes? Give students more time. *EdWeek.* https://www.edweek.org/leadership/opinion-want-to-improve-learning-outcomes-give-students-more-time/2021/03

Hanover Research. (2016). *Best practices in middle school program design: Prepared for Rockwood School District.* Author.

Harlacher, J. E., Sanford, A. K., & Nelson, N. (2014, May 15). Distinguishing between Tier 2 and Tier 3 instruction in order to support implementation of RTI. *Education Faculty Publications and Presentations, 132.* https://archives.pdx.edu/ds/psu/25582

Hattie, J. (2008). *Visible learning: A synthesis of over 800 meta-analyses relating to achievement.* SAGE.

Irmsher, K. (1996, March). Block scheduling. *Educational Management, 104.* http://www.eric.ed.gov/ERICDocs/data/ericdocs2/content_storage_01/0000000b/80/2a/25/a4.pdf

Ivok, L. (1944). *How to prepare the schedule for a secondary school.* Harvard University Press.

Ladd, G. W., & Ettekal, I. (2013, December). Peer-related loneliness across early to late adolescence: Normative trends, intra-individual trajectories, and links with depressive symptoms. *Journal of Adolescence, 36*(6), 1269–1282. https://doi.org/10.1016/j.adolescence.2013.05.004

Levenson, N. (2020). *Six shifts to improve special education and other interventions: A commonsense approach for school leaders.* Harvard Education Press.

Louisiana Department of Education. (2021, September 21). *Staffing and scheduling best practices guidance.* https://www.louisianabelieves.com/docs/default-source/academics/staffing-and-scheduling-guidance.pdf

Marzano, R. (2003). *What works in schools: Translating research into action.* ASCD.

Mendler, A. (2001). *Connecting with students.* ASCD.

Murray, J. (2013). *Access to rigor: Who gets it, who doesn't, and what does it mean.* https://fordhaminstitute.org/ohio/commentary/access-rigor-who-gets-it-who-doesnt-and-what-does-it-mean

National Assessment of Educational Progress. (2019a). *NAEP Report Card: 2019 NAEP Mathematics Assessment.* https://www.nationsreportcard.gov/highlights/mathematics/2019/

National Assessment of Educational Progress. (2019b). *NAEP Report Card: 2019 NAEP Reading Assessment.* https://www.nationsreportcard.gov/highlights/reading/2019/

National Institute of Child Health and Human Development, NIH, DHHS. (2000). *Report of the National Reading Panel: Teaching children to read* (00-4769). U.S. Government Printing Office.

O'Brien, E. M. (2006). *Key lessons: What research says about reorganizing school schedules.* Center for Public Education.

Pope, N. (2016). How the time of day affects productivity: Evidence from school schedules. *Review of Economics and Statistics, 98*(1), 1–11. https://direct.mit.edu/rest/article-abstract/98/1/1/58293/How-the-Time-of-Day-Affects-Productivity-Evidence

Reeves, P. M., Pun, W. H., & Chung, K. S. (2017). Influence of teacher collaboration on job satisfaction and student achievement. *Teaching and Teacher Education, 67*(8), 227–236.

Rettig, M., & Canady, R. L. (1999, March 1). The effects of block scheduling. *School Administrator, 56*(3), 14–16,18–20. https://www.aasa.org/schooladministratorarticle.aspx?id=14852

Reynolds, D. (2008). *How professional learning communities use student data for improving achievement*. University of Southern California, PhD dissertation.

Rodriguez-Delgado, C., Wang, F. K. W., Hays, G., & Chavez, R. (2021). *Schools across the country are struggling to find staff. Here's why.* https://www.pbs.org/newshour/education/schools-across-the-country-are-struggling-to-find-staff-heres-why

Schleifer, D., Rinehart, C., & Yanisch, T. (2017). *Teacher collaboration in perspective: A guide to research* [White paper]. Spencer Foundation and Public Agenda. https://files.eric.ed.gov/fulltext/ED591332.pdf

Schwartz, S. (2021, May 24). What's the best was to address unfinished learning? It's not remediation, study says. *Education Week*. https://www.edweek.org/teaching-learning/whats-the-best-way-to-address-unfinished-learning-its-not-remediation-study-says/2021/05

Snyder, T. D., & Dillow, S. A. (2011). *Digest of education statistics, 2010* (NCES 2011-01). National Center for Education Statistics, Institute of Education Sciences. https://nces.ed.gov/pubs2011/2011015.pdf

Sutcher, L., Darling-Hammond, L., & Carver-Thomas, D. (2016, September 15). *A coming crisis in teaching? Teacher supply, demand, and shortages in the U.S.* Learning Policy Institute. https://doi.org/10.54300/247.242

The College Board. (2022). *Student score distributions, AP Exams—May 2022.* https://apstudents.collegeboard.org/about-ap-scores/score-distributions

Theokas, C., & Saaris, R. (2013). *Finding America's missing AP and IB students*. The Education Trust. https://edtrust.org/wp-content/uploads/2013/10/Missing_Students.pdf

Underwood, S. (2018). *What is the evidence for an uninterrupted, 90-minute literacy instruction block?* https://educationnorthwest.org/sites/default/files/resources/uninterrupted-literacy-block-brief.pdf

Vaughn, S., Denton, C. A., & Fletcher, J. M. (2010). Why intensive interventions are necessary for Students with severe reading difficulties. *Psychology in the Schools, 47*(5), 432–444. https://doi.org/10.1002/pits.20481

Vaughn, S., Wanzek, J., Murray, C. S., & Roberts, G. (2012). *Intensive interventions for students struggling in reading and mathematics: A practice guide*. RMC Research Corporation, Center on Instruction.

West, M. R., & Schwerdt, G. (2012, February 15). The middle school plunge. *Education Next, 12*(2). https://www.educationnext.org/the-middle-school-plunge/

Wheaton, A. G., Ferro, G. A., & Croft, J. B. (2015, August 7). School start times for middle school and high school students—United States, 2011–12 school year. *Morbidity and Mortality Weekly Report, 64*(30), 809–813. https://www.cdc.gov/mmwr/preview/mmwrhtml/mm6430a1.htm

Zeiser, K., Scholz, C., & Cirks, V. (2018). *Maximizing student agency: Implementing and measuring student-centered learning practices*. American Institute for Research. https://files.eric.ed.gov/fulltext/ED592084.pdf

Zepeda, S., & Meyers, R. S. (2006). An analysis of research on block scheduling. *Review of Educational Research, 76*(1), 137–170.

Index

Note: The letter *f* following a page number denotes a figure.

About the Authors

Nathan Levenson is the president of New Solutions K12, an education consulting firm. For the past 15 years, he has helped school systems build strategic schedules, partnering with more than 250 school districts in 30 states.

Nate began his career in the private sector, but a passion for public education led to a career switch that included six years as a school board member; assistant superintendent for curriculum and instruction in Harvard, Massachusetts; and superintendent of Arlington (Mass.) Public Schools.

In Arlington, Nate helped champion an intensive reading program that reduced the number of students reading below grade level by two-thirds and revamped the district's special education services, which reduced the special education achievement gap by 66 percent. Neither initiative would have been possible without substantial shifts in schedules.

David James is a managing director at New Solutions K12, where he leads the firm's staffing and scheduling practice. He advises schools and districts nationally on how best to design, build, and manage school schedules that align to priorities and make the biggest impact for students. David designed and facilitates New Solutions K12's scheduling academy, which trains educators in how to approach scheduling strategically.

David began his career teaching 8th grade science in Chelsea (Mass.) Public Schools, where he helped implement a new block schedule and led his students to achieve the highest passing rate on the 8th grade science and technology state exam in district history. He went on to teach 6th grade science in Boston Public Schools and later planned and led the turnaround of a middle school in Lawrence (Mass.) Public Schools as part of state-led district improvement effort. In Lawrence, David helped design an innovative cohort schedule model and led the school to become the fastest-improving middle school in the state in its first year, with proficiency rates for 8th graders jumping from 36 percent to 61 percent in English language arts and from 13 percent to 48 percent in math.

Related ASCD Resources: School and District Leadership

At the time of publication, the following resources were available (ASCD stock numbers appear in parentheses):

Equity in Data: A Framework for What Counts in Schools by Andrew Knips, Sonya Lopez, Michael Savoy, and Kendall LaParo (#122021)

Dream Team: A Practical Playbook to Help Innovative Educators Change Schools by Aaron Tait and Dave Faulkner (#119022)

Fighting for Change in Your School: How to Avoid Fads and Focus on Substance by Harvey Alvy (#117001)

Leading Your School Toward Equity: A Practical Framework for Walking the Talk by Dwayne Chism (#123003)

Results Now 2.0: The Untapped Opportunities for Swift, Dramatic Gains in Achievement by Mike Schmoker (#123048)

Stop Leading, Start Building! Turn Your School into a Success Story with the People and Resources Your Already Have by Robyn R. Jackson (#121025)

The Teacher's Principal: How School Leaders Can Support and Motivate Their Teachers by Jen Schwanke (#122035)

Trauma-Sensitive School Leadership: Building a Learning Environment to Support Healing and Success by Bill Ziegler, Dave Ramage, Andrea Parson, and Justin Foster (#122013)

Uprooting Instructional Inequity: The Power of Inquiry-Based Professional Learning by Jill Harrison Berg (#121016)

For up-to-date information about ASCD resources, go to www.ascd.org. You can search the complete archives of *Educational Leadership* at www.ascd.org/el. To contact us, send an email to member@ascd.org or call 1-800-933-2723 or 703-578-9600.

WHOLE CHILD
TENETS

1 **HEALTHY**
Each student enters school healthy and learns about and practices a healthy lifestyle.

2 **SAFE**
Each student learns in an environment that is physically and emotionally safe for students and adults.

3 **ENGAGED**
Each student is actively engaged in learning and is connected to the school and broader community.

4 **SUPPORTED**
Each student has access to personalized learning and is supported by qualified, caring adults.

5 **CHALLENGED**
Each student is challenged academically and prepared for success in college or further study and for employment and participation in a global environment.

The ASCD Whole Child approach is an effort to transition from a focus on narrowly defined academic achievement to one that promotes the long-term development and success of all children. Through this approach, ASCD supports educators, families, community members, and policymakers as they move from a vision about educating the whole child to sustainable, collaborative actions.

It's Time for Strategic Scheduling relates to the **safe, engaged,** and **supported** tenets.

For more about the ASCD Whole Child approach, visit **www.ascd.org/wholechild.**